CONTENTS

"As a writer myself, I am always looking for a book to read that tells stories of everyday life about ordinary people that are full of humor. If you are like me, this book is perfect for you."

"I found this book so much fun to read that I felt compelled to read it in one go."

"If you have not lived or worked in the Indian corporate culture, this book will educate you while keeping you amused."

Prof. D. Yogi Goswami, in the Foreword

"In lot of ways, this book reminded me of short stories of Ruskin Bond."

"If there were a word, I would term this book as 'unputdownable' "

From a review of The Star is Born

"Nicely narrated the many events he is involved, with good humour."

From a review of Better Half With Golf

Jeeves Who Spoke to Flowers

And other humorous wonders of corporate
and work life in India

Rajeev Lal   **Bharti Sinha**

Copyright

DEDICATIONS

RAJEEV LAL

•   To my late father Dr. Kishori Saran Lal, a renowned historian. I inherited the interest in writing from him.

BHARTI SINHA

•   To my late uncles Hari Shankar Sinha, Krishna Shanker Sinha and father Madho Shanker Sinha who told great rib-tickling tales, and to whom rolling on the floor laughing signified appreciation;

•   To my mother Kumud Sinha, who forgot to tell me I was a girl and bravely allowed me to test convention.

ACKNOWLEDGEMENTS
Sincere thanks
to
Prof. D. Yogi Goswami
Inventor, Author, Entrepreneur and Educator
Distinguished Professor, University
of South Florida
and a globally renowned expert on solar energy
for writing a Foreword for this book.

RAJEEV LAL

I would like to acknowledge:

Every one of my co-workers and superiors who gave me the freedom to interact with them in a light-hearted way throughout my career. They are the inspiration and source of the stories I have written.

My co-author Bharti Sinha who came up with the idea of writing this book together

My granddaughter Trisha for creating the cover

and grandson Shaunak for paperback cover & technical help

BHARTI SINHA

I would like to acknowledge:

My bosses, colleagues and customers, who bore the brunt of my humour and continued to add to my learning;

Sunoor Verma without whose merciless prodding and deluded faith these stories would have remained in the recesses of my memory.

My late brother Neeraj Sinha - who was the test bed for refining my humour and swiftness of repartee – the sibling with whom it was always party time, and who asked me when I proudly gave him my very first visiting card with the designation "Officer on Special Duty" – "So what special duties do you perform" – I miss you, my sibling, friend and strongest critic!

And last, my co-author Rajeev Lal, for suffering my procrastination, laziness and sheer bloody-mindedness. You are a saint!

Illustrations by Priyanka Abbott

Also by Rajeev Lal

A Star is Born
Better Half With Golf

FOREWORD

Prof. Yogi D. Goswami

As a writer myself, I am always looking for a book to read that tells stories of everyday life about ordinary people that are full of humor. If you are like me, this book is perfect for you. It gives you a peek into certain aspects of the Indian corporate culture mixed with the local culture. It is written in an engaging style to the point that once you start reading, you cannot put it down until you finish reading all of it. I have myself published 23 books and more than 400 papers on science and technology, which are all important but quite boring to read. However, I found this book so much fun to read that I felt compelled to read it in one go. I have known the author, Rajeev Lal, as a friend and an engineering college classmate from 1964 to 1969. Although I have not met Bharti Sinha, the co-author, after reading her stories in the book, I feel that I know her and will enjoy listening to her stories in person anytime.

The co-authors, Rajeev Lal and Bharti Sinha couldn't be more different in their writing styles, but with one important common trait; they both describe their experiences with their corporate colleagues in a captivating and humorous style. Their stories show that they themselves had a lot of fun at the expense of their colleagues and sometimes even at their own expense. I found their different writing styles even more interesting for my reading since they have alternated their stories in the book. Going from one style to the other and from one type of corporate story to another, made it really fun to read.

Rajeev starts with a story of his interview that led to his first job as an industrial engineer right out of the engineering college. I am sure you will enjoy reading how the interview went. Here you can feel how much fun Rajeev has, describing his conversations with the interviewers and the motivations of some of the interviewers that were totally unrelated to the interview. The time frame of this story is sometime around 1970. Rajeev asked the head of the interviewing team if they had any computers in their company, since Rajeev was advised that he would impress the interviewer if he asked some questions. The hilarious part of this story is that the interviewer told an employee to show Rajeev the hundreds of computers in another part of the company and what Rajeev saw there. You have to read the book to find the answer yourself, that I am sure you will enjoy.

Bharti has written about her own funny experiences in her corporate sales career. I will just mention one, where she describes a residential training program of a team of 15 salespersons. The group consists of a wide range of persons from a "Mama's boy" to those who could sell anything to anyone. She focused the story on SS, the sheltered "Mama's boy", who is going through the training while going home to his mother every evening for a change of clothes. SS is innocent, trusting and unaware of the wicked ways of the world, so everyone else is having fun at his expense. As you can imagine the two weeks of training led to a number of funny incidents where everyone else had fun at his expense. You have to read all of those incidents in the book in the fascinating way Bharti describes them.

An amusing aspect of the contemporary Indian culture is to understand what is implied but never said. There are many instances in the stories where you have to understand what is implied. The authors give you an insight into what was left unsaid. If you are of Indian origin and have lived and worked in the Indian corporate culture, you will be able to identify with the characters and the stories. If, on the other hand, you have not lived or worked in the Indian corporate culture, this book will educate you while keeping you amused.

I have enjoyed reading the book immensely and

am eagerly waiting for their next one.

D. Yogi Goswami, Ph.D.

Distinguished University Professor
Director, Clean Energy Research Center,
University of South Florida, Tampa, Florida, USA
Editor-in-Chief, *Solar Compass*, Journal of the
International Solar Alliance
Emeritus Editor-in-Chief, *Solar Energy*, Journal of
the International Solar Energy Society

PREFACE

It started in the nineteen fifties, gained momentum in the sixties and seventies and became a flood thereafter. Students from India went to US, Canada, Europe, Australia etc. and joined professional courses in the universities there. After completing their courses, they took up jobs within those countries and settled down there. Doctors, engineers and others sought employment in these developed countries.

Over a period these people helped their brothers, sisters, cousins and friends to follow suit, which has today created a powerhouse of an Indian diaspora, who influence the highest echelons of society in these countries.

Their intellectual acumen and talent, coupled with hard work and discipline has over the decades, earned them respect within the countries they adopted. A large number of people of Indian origin achieved and continue to reach great heights and success. Testimony to this is evidenced in many global corporations like Google, IBM, Microsoft and Twitter being headed by them. Apart from this Indian origin doctors, engineers, scientists, economists, professors and software developers are well respected for their contribution across the globe.

However, the talent that migrated was a miniscule compared to the thousands who stayed home in India. These brave souls thrived braving strong headwinds - a legacy of the erstwhile British Raj combined with the conservative Indian mindset; such as non-recognition of good work, workplace politics, nepotism, limited opportunities, and other forms of corporate malaise.

Over the years, with corporate India becoming more integrated with the international work culture, this situation has improved dramatically.

The Information Technology revolution has since led to a quantum growth, offering better opportunities and earnings for many even within India, as well as positively impacting the work-place environment. Hierarchy, age and longevity of experience are no longer considered primary assets for career progression – ability and talent are today the key factors. And importantly workplaces also started opening up from being a man's domain, to include women, and to offer opportunities at senior executive levels and in board rooms.

This has brought about significant transformation in the Indian marketplace as well as how we are viewed in the more developed world. In recent years the reverse migration, signalled with a handful of Indians who had left the country at a young age to look for greener pastures coming back to serve in their homeland, has also served as a catalyst to bring about this perception.

Further, over the past decade and half, India and China have emerged as defining destinations for top level positions in the Western world, and so several "C" level aspirants in companies in these developed countries are angling for a stint of a few years here. This trend did dampen a little during the pandemic but the revival has started again, with India now taking an edge over China as a more favoured destination today.

This book has been the penning down of real and could-have-been-real experiences by the two of us, who are the authors of this book. A bit about us – I, Rajeev Lal, an engineer from the prestigious Delhi College of Engineering, University of Delhi, having lived this story from the 70s onwards, when the use of computers in corporate India started proliferating, have been both a witness as well as a participant in ushering in the computer revolution in the country.

And I, Bharti Sinha, on the other hand, have a B.A. Honours degree as well as Masters' degree in English Literature from Lady Shri Ram College for Women, University of Delhi. Let me at the outset frankly confess that maths stumps me. With these qualifications, least suitable for a career in the technology space, I started out in the '80s when women were still a scarce entity in the corporate world. Against the odds, I ended up as part of the pioneering team who set out to defy the conventional opinion of a woman's role in corporates and redefine what women could do. To add to the measure of difficulty, I was plummeted onto the centre-stage in the world of technology.

Drawing from different stages of corporate evolution, educational qualifications and of course genders, both of us have charted our own paths, experiencing challenges, extraordinary successes, devastating failures and at times heartbreaks. On looking back, we feel that with no trodden path to follow, we have surprisingly navigated all these with élan.

In this book, we have tried to give you a glimpse into the personal stories of real people. In doing so we are sharing nuggets from our experiences, as well as candid admissions of the work life adventures we have faced, and how much fun one could find in each day.

After several decades of working and growing, and sometimes competing, in separate companies, the two of us also ended up working together for some years in the same information technology company.

Since both of us have a propensity to use humour

in various situations, including happenings at the workplace, and also have the ability to laugh at ourselves, we believe that all the stories told here will bring a smile as well as irrepressible laughter to you, dear readers.

All our stories are narrated in a lighter vein to make for enjoyable reading. We hope that these stories will convince readers that working in India is as much fun as working anywhere else in the world. The text is interspersed with sentences in *italics* that highlight the traits of Indians.

A small mention about our styles. You will find our individual experiences and perspectives reflected in our stories.

Rajeev writes in simple day to day English which is easy flowing and conversational. His clarity of thought, apt choice of the right word and the straight, uncomplicated storyline, lend for universal appeal and make his stories easy to understand.

Bharti's language is distinctive and reflects the influence on her of British humour, as espoused by P.G. Wodehouse, Gerald Durrell and others in that wake. She has interspersed some sentences in the Indian language Hindi for effect. While at times her stories veer on being a bit wicked, her self-deprecating style and ability to be equally critical of her own foibles, ensures that her stories entertain.

Author's name is mentioned after the title in each chapter.

The stories span a period of five decades and are drawn from various parts of India. A lot has changed in India over the years and yet the characters and happenings in the stories can still be found. Some towns and cities have grown and developed beyond expectations. Roads have improved and highways connect many parts of the country. Still, jaywalkers, stray animals and dangerous potholes are a common sight on roads in many places.

For the upper middle class, life in India is comparatively more comfortable than in the West. The offices here can now compare with the best anywhere in the world. Telecom efficiency and dropping costs have enabled virtual distances to shrink, and travel costs and facilities becoming affordable have given wing to the middle class. Today, it is a commonplace sight to see Indian tourists rubbing shoulders with the American and Japanese travellers anywhere in the world. Yes, the world has changed, but to know just how much, this will book will shed a light.

As many of these stories are true, the names of people have been changed in order that retribution cannot be meted out. However, the experiences are fairly universal and so may seem familiar to many.

We hope that this book will encourage Indian

professionals to open up and share more such stories and convince everyone that working in India is fun!

Rajeev Lal   Bharti Sinha

https://www.linkedin.com/in/rajeev-lal-1926681
https://www.linkedin.com/in/bharti-sinha/

June 2022

THE INTERVIEW

Rajeev Lal

Fresh from the college, in 1970 I got an interview call for a position in the Industrial Engineering Department of a large steel mill in eastern India. I had completed my mechanical engineering course from a prestigious institute in Delhi securing a First Class degree, but jobs eluded us by the time we passed out. They were like beautiful girls. Many of us ran after each one, and everyone went after many in the hope that one will choose us. Lucky were those few who got chosen by one.

I had completed my mechanical engineering course from a prestigious institute in Delhi securing a First Class degree, but jobs eluded us by the time we passed out.
They were like beautiful girls. Many of us ran after each one, and everyone went after many in the hope that one will choose us.

I travelled by train for the interview. It took about twenty-four hours to reach the place by train from Delhi. I was in the second-class sleeper coach, which had six wooden berths in each coupe.

The berths were painted light brown. The coupe was open from the side that had the passage for the compartment. It was full, with five fellow passengers seated on the two long lower berths facing each other. With three tiers, at night six people could sleep in the coupé with the middle berths raised.

As the passengers exchanged pleasantries and started introducing each other, one of them turned out to be an engineer in his forties. He was working in the Public Works Department of the government and was posted in the area where I was going for my interview.

"I am Er. Prasad from the PWD", he introduced himself.

There was a popular movement at that time amongst engineers to develop an identity as a distinct group of professionals, and many of them had started using the salutation "Er". for identifying themselves as Engineers. It had its beginnings in Germany, where the practice I believe was quite common. It was not customary for government officers to carry visiting cards those days. Anyway, an ordinary second class train compartment was the last place worthy of a ceremonial exchange of cards with strangers.

Er. Prasad sounded exuberant, interested in knowing everyone around. His face lit up when I told him that I had graduated as an engineer recently.

After some time both of us opened up. He had been a brilliant student, and from the time he decided to study engineering, he was sure that he would work in the PWD. It seemed that this was a common ambition for engineers in Bihar, his home state.

"There is no stress and enough money, and contractors are at one's beck and call for any needs" he said. "One gets an official Jeep, so transport is never a problem".

Personal cars were a luxury for the middle class those days in India. Er. Prasad was a great believer in the Engineering fraternity, and I could make out that he wanted to go out of his way to help me, a fellow engineer looking for a job. He gave me a detailed background of the company where I was going for my interview.

"I can arrange for you to stay at Ethi for the two days that you have to be there. It is close to the place where you have to go for interview", he told me after we had spent some time talking together. With a pause, he added that I could even eat at Ethi, pronounced *aiyethi*, which was close to Ethi and quite cheap.

I was a bit perplexed by his frequent use of the word "Ethi", realising that my first assumption that Ethi was the name of a main locality was incorrect. As I heard some more conversations amongst the fellow travellers, I realised that Ethi is a frequently used common noun in the eastern Indian state of Bihar. It can mean a place, a thing or a person depending on the context.

I shuddered at the thought of the misunderstandings that this simple word had the potential to create, especially amongst the uninitiated.

It transpired that in this case Ethi was the PWD inspection bungalow.

The train was not too late and we reached in the evening. Er. Prasad was kind enough to drop me at the inspection bungalow in the Jeep that had come to pick him up from the railway station. His driver was well trained to look after guests. He put my bag in the Jeep and helped me climb into it.

The rear seat of a Jeep, covered with tarpaulin on the top and the sides, is not the best for taking in the sights and understanding the directions in a new town. It is the view one will get if one managed to jog sideways.

We reached the PWD Inspection Bungalow in less than half an hour, driving through reasonably good and wide roads, which were lined on both sides with tall trees as we came nearer to the destination. The town was definitely better planned and much better maintained than most towns I had seen in India. I was struck by the cleanliness of the roads.

We reached a single storey building with a boundary wall all around it. A blue rectangular sign board, in the standard design used for government offices and buildings, announced "PWD Inspection Bungalow" in white letters. It was fixed on two wooden poles.

A gatekeeper opened the wooden gate with a crisp salute and the Jeep went over a set of pipes laid in parallel, joined together by a few steel girders welded across them. I thought it was a speed breaker, but learnt later that a drain is made at the gate and then bridged with these pipes to prevent snakes, cows and buffalos making an entry through the gate meant for human beings.

We drove through a sizeable walled compound and the Jeep stopped in the arched portico.

I had seen some government inspection bungalows in the past and this one was no different. It was well maintained and quite clean. The building was painted crimson on the outside like the boundary wall and had a tiled roof. The walls inside were painted white with lime, having a tinge of ultramarine blue.

The caretaker greeted Er. Prasad with extreme reverence. He in turn told the caretaker that I would stay there for two nights and made some entries in the log book kept on a dark brown wooden table at the entrance of the hall. The small table had outlived its life; the legs wobbled as Er.

Prasad wrote in the book. It was difficult to make out whether the dark brown colour was a remnant of the polish or was the colour of the wood itself.

Er. Prasad asked me to make the nominal payment calculated as per standard charges at the time of leaving. He also told me that instead of trying to look around in the town, I could get very good food at reasonable prices at the hotel run by the company where I was going for the interview. The hotel was located just opposite the inspection bungalow and was the best in the city.

I felt grateful to this fellow engineer and was relieved at having finally unravelled the mystery behind the ubiquitous Ethi. I noted his name, address and telephone number on a piece of paper. I thanked him profusely, and he wished me good luck in getting the job.

As he left, the caretaker took my suitcase, which had been brought down by the driver, and ushered me into the room where I was to stay. I gave him a small tip. He looked surprised, and I noticed a muted smile on his face. Obviously he wasn't getting tips often as the Inspection Bungalow was mostly used by government officers.

Helping strangers is quite common in India

After Er. Prasad left and I had settled down in my room, I had a bath and some rest. I was feeling nice and refreshed, and by 8 p.m. I was hungry. I walked up to the hotel across the road in front of the inspection bungalow for dinner.

It was a well-lit white building, very elegant and nicely maintained. The corridors had granite floors and other areas had marble floors. The dining room was adjacent to the reception, and a liveried waiter escorted me to a table as I entered it. It was filled with simple square tables spaced out well, covered with crisp white tablecloths and had four chairs for each one. The furniture and setting was functional and elegant, not lavish.

Not even half the tables in the dining hall were occupied. Most of the diners looked to be residents in the hotel on business trips. There were only two couples at two different tables. The atmosphere was serene, the conversations were soft and muted. Some of the diners looked up casually with a frown – "What is a youngster looking like a student doing here alone?"

An elegant typed menu card in a German silver stand with "Dinner" as its heading adorned the centre of the table. It mentioned the four courses – soup, starters, main course and dessert. After a long and tiring train journey with no good food, the sumptuous looking menu was mouth-watering. The starters and main course included kebabs, curries, pulao etc.; the dessert was ice-cream – chocolate, vanilla or strawberry.

"Dinner – Rs. 8" was typed at the bottom. The price looked too good for the menu; the hotel was owned and run by the company where I was attending the interview, and it was obvious that it was heavily subsidised.

Suddenly I became victim of the Indian middle-class frugality which springs up wherever it is least needed. Overcome by the thought that I was unemployed and not entitled to luxury, I decided to do still better and save some money for my father.

"Can I have something else, some simple food?", I asked the waiter as he came to check if he could bring the soup. It took me some courage to say it, but I did it smoothly. "Why not, Sir?", he said – having been trained to exhibit impeccable manners and put all kinds of customers at ease.

"I would like to have some dal (lentils), a dry vegetable and chapattis", I told him. "Of course, Sir. Would you like some dry bhindi (Lady's Finger)?", he asked. "Yes that will be fine", I said and waited for my meal, elated that I had resisted the temptation to splurge, acted with confidence in a situation that had made me nervous and saved some money.

Many Indians are frugal, bordering on being misers. The younger generation is turning out to be different

After some time the waiter brought piping hot dal, with nicely fried bhindi and chapattis (Indian bread, like tortillas). He served the dal in a small bowl and the vegetable in my plate. Two chapattis were there in a basket, which the waiter refilled once.

The food was delicious, and I ate well. When I signalled to the waiter that no more chapattis were needed, he waited for me to finish and then cleared the plates. He then brought a finger bowl with warm water and a slice of lemon. The finger bowl was also of white metal, polished and kept neatly on a plate.

"Which flavour of ice cream will you like, Sir?", the waiter asked as he picked up the finger bowl after I had finished. "No thanks. I do not feel like having a dessert. Please get me my bill", I told him. I was sure that the simple meal that I had ordered would cost half of the standard dinner charge. I was already running my fingers on a five rupee note in my pocket to settle the bill including the tip.

The waiter brought the bill – it was for eight rupees. "There must be some mistake", I picked up courage again and said "this bill is for the standard dinner menu". "There is a fixed dinner charge, Sir, even if you choose to have a something else instead of the standard menu", he said in a matter of fact way.

I was shaken and did not know what to say or do. I simply took out a ten rupee note and kept it in the folder. "At least get me a strawberry ice cream" – I was tempted to shout after the waiter as he walked away. Good sense prevailed on me and I quietly came out of the dining room.

As I walked back I kept cursing myself for being so foolish as to not even check how an alternate menu will be charged. I thought of the hot soup, nice kebabs and a good dessert that I had been deprived of and on top of it paid the full dinner charge in the end.

Indians hesitate to ask questions
– and assume a lot

Even the nice breeze and the tall trees all around could not elevate my depressed mood. I continued to berate myself as I lay down to sleep. I kept turning and tossing, agonizing at my blunder for some time.

Thankfully the train journey had made me tired, and I dozed off after a few minutes. By that time I had already figured out how I would describe the nice dinner at the hotel to others based on the menu, giving them no clue of my folly.

I got up in the morning fully refreshed, but the agony of the blunder over dinner on the previous night had not gone away. I got dressed, collected and checked the papers that I had to carry for the interview and went to the company's office where the interviews were to be held. It was not very far, and the caretaker gave me good directions.

There were about 20 candidates called for interviews that day. I was wearing a suit and found only two others in similar attire. All the others were in shirts and trousers, not even sporting a tie. I noticed that people working in the company were also not wearing any ties. I felt a little out of place, more so as many company employees glanced at me curiously as they walked by. Nothing could be done about it, so I decided to just ignore my overdressing.

The day started well. My spirits started rising as I fared well in the first interview, with the Deputy Chief Industrial Engineer. At the end I was asked to wait along with five others and the rest were asked to collect their reimbursements of travel expenses from the Accounts department and leave.

All those asked to wait were taken for a simple lunch in the cafeteria. Ironically it consisted of dal, fried bhindi, chapattis, potato curry and rice. The cafeteria was fairly large and one had to take a rectangular steel plate having small compartments and pick up the food from the buffet laid out. After finishing our food, we kept the used plates in racks kept near the exit like all others.

The final interview post-lunch had a panel of five persons seated in a row across the table, while I cowered on a simple armless chair on the other side. The tone of the interview was set by the Chief Industrial Engineer Mr. Karunakaran. He looked at me from head to toe, and smiled faintly, amused to see me wearing a suit. He spoke in a soft but firm tone, and there was pin-drop silence when he spoke.

He was the first to ask some questions. As soon as he put one, the other panel members looked at him with a deference that someone who had asked the most intelligent question in the world deserved. His demeanour put the candidate at ease, and I overcame my fear and started answering the questions. After he finished asking the questions, he signalled to the other panel members. They started putting questions to me one by one.

As soon as they finished asking a question, they looked at the Chief, Mr. Karunakaran. It was obvious that they worked under him. They wanted to confirm through his expression whether he was impressed by the question or at least approved of it.

The Chief was a past master at conducting interviews and sat with a straight expressionless face. This resulted in the questioner getting more anxious than the candidate. While Mr. Karunakaran carefully listened when I answered his questions, the others did not seem interested in the answers to theirs – they were looking at Mr. Karunakaran all the time when I answered.

Sycophancy and the urge to impress others are common traits in Indians

The interview was finally over, which I understood when Mr. Karunakaran asked me if I had any questions. The books I had read on successful interviews all instructed that this opportunity had to be grabbed. Very often the question asked determined whether one is selected or not, they said.

I was fully prepared and asked "Sir, do you have computers in your department? I worked on a computer in my university, and will be very happy if I can get an opportunity to use one here too, if I am selected".

The last phrase was also as per the emphasis in the books – never give an impression that you are assuming that you have been selected. Mr. Karunakaran replied "Of course, we have a large number of computers". I could again see a faint smile on his lips as he said it.

I had a bigger smile on my face, said "Thank you, Sir", loudly and started getting up from my seat. Mr. Karunakaran nodded his head, which I surmised meant that I could go. I walked a couple of steps backward, gave a Japanese bow to the panel and said "thank you" again. I then slowly exited the room.

I was selected. It was a large company and it took time for them to issue the appointment letter and complete other formalities. The appointment letter ran through four pages, the last one being the letter of acceptance. The draft of a three-page service bond that I was required to execute at the time of joining was attached with the appointment letter. Another two page letter informed me that I was entitled to shared bachelor accommodation at the time of joining, and the terms of the accommodation that would be made available.

I joined the company after a month. I just needed to make arrangements for a couple of days stay on reaching the place. I was at first tempted to write to Er. Prasad requesting him for help in staying at the inspection bungalow for two days but later gave up the idea. I was now going to work in a good company and could avoid taking advantage of government accommodation.

The introductory note that accompanied the appointment letter had a list of hotels in the town. I decided to stay in one of them. This also saved me from the embarrassment of going back to the hotel opposite the inspection bungalow and getting reminded of the blunder that I had committed there while having dinner on my maiden visit.

It did not take time to realise that the company I joined was a very hierarchical organization. Most of the communication was one way; we listened to our superiors and quietly did what we were asked to. Periodic dressing down by the superiors ensured that we did not go wayward, and understood who we owed our existence to. One had to think twice before opening one's mouth, let alone asking any questions.

The new batch of Industrial Engineers had a monthly meeting with the Chief Industrial Engineer. It was only in the third meeting when I picked up the courage to ask Mr. Karunakaran about the computers.

He had a sharp memory. "Yes, Yes. I remember. You had asked about computers in your interview. Natraj, please take this boy to our computers tomorrow", he ordered my immediate boss.

Next morning at around 11 a.m. Natraj called me and asked me to accompany him on the pillion of his light blue Vespa scooter. It was old and noisy. He drove close to the main gate where some of the oldest buildings in the factory were located and parked his scooter next to one.

I followed him into a white coloured building with a small door for entrance and a very high ceiling. There was a wooden mezzanine floor in the part that we entered. An old wooden staircase led to it. The stairs creaked as we walked up. They ended into a large hall lit brightly with tube lights on the ceiling, and rows of tables as far as one could see.

Each table had a machine which looked like a heavy typewriter, and people sitting at the tables were continuously hammering at the keys. Most of them seemed to be in their fifties. Only some of them looked up and hesitatingly smiled at Natraj, who acknowledged their greeting with a nod through an imperceptible movement of the head. The clicks of the keys made the only noise, and it created the feeling of some wonky tapping music being played by amateurs.

"The machines you see are Comptometers", Natraj told me. "and the people working on them are Computers. They are entering the work details of the employees and computing their incentive".

The machine-like behaviour of the people justified their designation. I was in a state of shock, almost in a trance. I felt that I will faint. I wanted to work on a computer, not become one. My dreams of working on a computer were completely shattered. I said nothing while Natraj looked at me expectantly, waiting for me to utter a cry of joy for having finally seen the computers.

I realised that courtesy required me to say something, and came back to the real world. "Thanks for bringing me here, Sir. How many computers do we have?" were the only words I could utter with some effort.

"About a hundred", he replied.

We quietly came down the rickety staircase and he drove me back to our office. Crestfallen, I went back to join my team.

Natraj would have immediately informed Mr. Karunakaran of having dutifully carried out the instructions given to him the previous day. I am sure Mr. Karunakaran would have chuckled on getting the update and on my shock and silent suffering.

> *Indian executives are generally honest but can use their intelligence to take you for a ride without your having the slightest clue*

But as luck would have it, I did have the last laugh. Within a year of joining I was selected for the position of Programmer and transferred to the EDP (Electronic Data Processing) Department within the Company. Mr. Karunakaran unsuccessfully opposed the transfer.

I was thrilled, my dream had come true. I felt a bit let down though when, due to sudden exit of the EDP Manager, the charge of the department was given for a few months to the Deputy General Manager (Typing and Mailing).

SETTING THE SHOW-OFF STRAIGHT

Bharti Sinha

In every organization, especially in the Sales department, you find some bumptious loudmouths who have a constantly rolling-forward closure date for forecasted deals. Somehow, these characters also manage to ensure that even "assured" orders get postponed or lost by confusing clients as well their companies so much that it takes extraordinary effort to retrieve these, if at all!

In every organization, especially in the Sales department, you find some bumptious loudmouths who have a constantly rolling-forward closure date for forecasted deals.

One such embodiment of tactless and abrasive behaviour was Rakesh Nagpal, or Rocky, as he called himself. "Hi, I'm Rocky, you know?...

Sylvester, you know?" he would announce as he butted his way into serious conversations with his big fat hand outstretched to grab the unwary. A rude colleague in fact retorted with "No, I don't know, but don't ya mean, Sanju?", referring to the infamous Bollywood actor's debut character.

Well, Rocky entered the computer company I worked in due to an erroneous selection and had to be suffered for at least a year before his lack of performance led to a swift and long-awaited welcome exit.

Within a week of joining, he managed to make himself thoroughly disliked by everyone from the office peon to the rest of his colleagues in the regional office. In the first month, with glib talk he borrowed significant amounts of money from everyone in the office. Unfortunately this ensured that no one would complain about his work, for his dismissal would also result in the money loaned disappearing forever. We discovered this much later when we compared notes.

In the very first monthly sales review, to our disgust and the manager's delight, Rocky managed to show so many prospective clients that all of us got a roasting for being lazy and inefficient. This paragon of hard and sincere toil was held up before our jealous eyes as a role model to emulate! He became the blue-eyed boy.

With the long gestation cycles that the sales of the

computerised solutions typically have in India, he could ingeniously pull the wool over the bosses' eyes by constantly dropping names of prospects and dates for milestones. The latter would somehow always see last minute cancellations or postponements, but it took a while before this raised any alarm.

This was not because the bosses were incompetent, but rather due to the fairly swift attrition of the leadership seeing a change of two to three managers in the space of around six months. This naturally created enough laxity to allow Rocky to survive long enough without actually getting a genuine prospect.

At last he managed to get one. This spelt a large multi-million rupee deal and meant a lot of time was required to be spent out of office on the calls. However, ironically, the customer had taken a king-sized dislike to Rocky and his cocky ways, especially since all his queries remained unaddressed. This client was an existing user of our company's services, so he had clearly decided that the order would be given to us. However, to do so, he still needed to put up a detailed execution plan with clearly definable milestones for deliverables in order to get the purchase approved internally and release the formal Purchase Order.

He had repeatedly tried to explain what he wanted and even handed over the formats in which he wanted the information to be presented, but

Rocky being Rocky, kept saying, "Got it, don't worry, boss" while obviously not understanding anything at all! This naturally led to a considerable amount of frustration and heartburn on the client's end, of which Rocky remained, in true inimitable Rocky style, obtusely and blissfully unaware.

Finally, one fateful morning, driven to desperation, the client decided that the mountain must come to Mohammed. He came to our office, just in time to catch us all, sans Rocky who was not famed for his "early bird" ways, while we were grabbing our morning cuppa before we all went forth in different directions to woo our respective prospective clients. As the client looked at us with feeble hope flickering in his drawn and harried face, our hearts went out to him.

That he had been facing trying times was no news to us, for even our limited interactions with Rocky always left us purple-faced and breathing heavily. To be condemned for no fault of his, to an unresponsive bloke such as Rocky, must have seemed like premature purgatory on earth. Without doubt he must have wondered whether the sins in his past life were colossal enough to merit this!

In deference to an existing customer, a couple of us volunteered to cancel our meetings for the day to help him out, at least until, as we imagined, Rocky decided to make his appearance in the office. I must admit that the client was one of the most thorough and systematic professionals and his efforts left us little to do, except some minor tweaking and fine tuning. After that it only required the effort estimations and costing to be worked out and a formal proposal to be generated.

All this we managed to accomplish in less than five hours, and we were able to then relax and have a well-deserved, albeit late, lunch. We also invited the now immensely grateful and relieved client, and he was pleased to join. Needless to say, in all this the one entity missing in action was Rocky!

Somehow, it was amazing that Rocky had an unerring instinct to stay away from any place where work was being done and only materialised when it was all over (although it was fortuitous that he had not shown up thus far, for it was certain that nothing would have been accomplished had he been around to "contribute"). We were, to put it mildly, extremely peeved at having to bail him out. This led us to jointly plan to wreak retribution on his head, ably and stoutly supported by the client, who was also game to get a bit of his own back at Rocky after having been tested and tortured for so long.

Hence, we all decided not to inform Rocky that in his absence, all had been done and the order was only a week away from being released.

The client too, kept us informed of the progress

and was happily able to get the Purchase Order and the cheque for advance ready on the fateful morning of our monthly sales review. During all this time, the client had kept Rocky at bay and remained unavailable for telephonic or face-to-face contact. It would all be a mystery to Rocky, as we had done all his work. We were now convinced, there was only one serious prospect for Rocky, who was still "extremely busy" making sales calls all day, to Lord knows which prospective client who refused to commit!

Anyway, to get back to our story, the client was good enough to send across the order and cheque personally to the two of us who had worked on the proposal, first thing that morning, ahead of the review. Hence, when the review started, the order, the cheque and the background were all available with our Regional head. Needless to say, Rocky was ready with his plausible tales of orders in the sky about to drop like manna into his lap – "Any day now, boss – just wait!"

Boss, who had just about had enough, was mentally gnashing his teeth and possibly delaying his onslaught while he debated on the best mode of attack, oscillating, no doubt between drawing and quartering Rocky, or dancing on his premature grave in hobnailed boots.

Before he could come to a decision, however, Rocky obliged by giving him a dream opening. Sighing deeply, our hero declared that he thought the only way the customer would be enticed into signing on the dotted line was if a fully paid holiday for a whole week, Sundays included, to Goa was arranged by the company for the IT head and his family (accompanied of course by Rocky and spouse).

"Mark it down to marketing expenses, boss", Rocky went on, while at the same time, enumerating the cost elements – (airfare, hotel stay – "must be 5-star deluxe, Sir; can't be stingy, can we?" – a car – "air conditioned, luxury" – "that's all, except, how do we account for the liquor – you do know he is a border-line alcoholic, right?"). As his favourite tipple was Johnny Walker, it required the services of a high-class bootlegger.

Widening nostrils and laboured breathing were the only giveaways that Boss, as he looked at Rocky, planned to treat us to the interesting times that were to come very soon. He shared the problem of being unable to approve such expenses in advance since "top management" was likely to view this as possible "attempt to bribe". However, should Rocky, "accidentally, mind you", be on holiday with his spouse, after taking necessary approvals for a holiday, and be "forced to take care of these expenses", then, on his return, all such expenses could be submitted in several vouchers for business and client entertainment expenses.

Boss would approve them. The financial dilemma on how to fund this was also helpfully sorted out by advising Rocky to take a salary advance, "which would be settled when the claims were presented".

Rocky was clearly overwhelmed with joy, and rushed, barely containing his whoops of sheer delight, as he ran to the reception to call his spouse and inform her to start packing as they were leaving coming Sunday morning for Goa. "Had boss agreed? Of course he had, and promised unlimited expenses for the trip, so take out that nice red with yellow polka dot swim suit for this second honeymoon!"

Well, while Rocky was on his way to splurging away his next month's salary, Boss was prodding us to use that week's reprieve to follow up and check on the other "hot" prospects that Rocky had been flaunting month on month. Needless to say that pricking that particular balloon was a mere formality when Rocky returned completely broke, armed with some real and some fake bills. The following week he had a new role – to break his back on some new 24 × 7 market research and mailer campaign that was personally monitored on an hourly basis by Boss.

As life chugged on for the next two months, we became used to the sorry sight of a bedraggled and drooping Rocky as the first thing each morning and last thing each evening. In fact, Rocky became an accepted fixture outside Boss's room, mostly silent, but with an occasional bleating "Yes, Boss … coming, Boss … almost done, Boss" as the only signs that he still had a voice!

When he eventually found himself ousted from the company, many of the folk only realised he had left when they tried to locate him, hoping for a return of their long, (and now, permanently), overdue loans!

None of us ever saw Rocky again, but I am sure, wherever he is, he must still be pulling the wool over other eyes as he fluidly entices unsuspecting new entrants into improving his liquidity before he exits their lives to target new wallets!

Indians hesitate in saying no, even to office colleagues borrowing money

JEEVES WHO SPOKE TO FLOWERS

Rajeev Lal

The steel mill had its own residential township. Housing was intended to be provided for all – managers and workers. However, as the company grew, the additional houses built could not match the demand. A few private housing colonies had come up. These were far away from the township, dwellings that were generally of poor quality and were expensive. Roads connecting them to the township were in very bad shape. As lack of accommodation was coming in the way of good candidates joining the company, young engineers were given bachelor accommodation.

I was allotted an old two-bedroom single-storied house. The houses were constructed in a row like barracks and were originally allotted to factory workers. I was to share it with another engineer. In my case he was with the company already for a year and was staying in the house when I moved in. Mervin D'Souza was a Catholic, six feet tall with an athletic built. He was born and brought up in Bombay (Mumbai now).

Mervin drove a Java motorbike, which had a single long, shiny leather seat. Those who have ridden Java bikes know that they always jumped off at start. Mervin added a thrill to it by starting with the accelerator raced. Almost every pillion rider on his bike had slipped and fallen off at least once. Mervin used to drive with large glasses and considered it below his dignity to ever look back. If one had the misfortune of slipping out of the pillion, he or she would have to find his or her own way. Mervin would be the last one to know of it.

At times this happened at traffic signals. The other frequent occurrence was that Mervin would miss the turn to our colony while returning at night from parties after a couple of drinks. It was not that he did not know where to turn, but most of the time his speed did not allow for a turn to be made. The U-turn was quite far, but it was a good ride in the nice breeze that was mostly there at night. Mervin also had a booming voice and his presence could be felt from quite some distance.

The house was in a nice quiet colony, the road was lined with tall trees. Each house had a garden and lawn in front and a courtyard at the back, privileges one can have only in a small town. It was common for the resident bachelors to keep a full-time servant. Mervin had a sixteen-year-old boy named Kabul. He had come from a village a couple of hundred miles from the township.

Kabul spoke only the local dialect of his village, with Hindi and Bengali words mixed in it. Mervin could speak only in English, with some words of the Bombay Hindi thrown in. None of these words were in Kabul's vocabulary. Yet on the first day itself I realised that Mervin and Kabul were able to communicate well and understand each other – each one speaking in his own language. One could feel that they bonded well.

Kabul's village was located in a region highly influenced by Naxalism, a movement in some parts of India that propagates violent revolution for social change. He was thus conscious of his rights and entitlements, and did not keep it a secret. His stare could create a scare. But Mervin was his hero. He tried to copy Mervin, and at the same time would do anything Mervin told him to.

Very soon I realised that this was a special relationship, and I could not expect Kabul to behave the same way with me or others. Kabul had the stubbornness of a youngster in his early teens. He was not given to listening to others easily, and was willing to get into an argument or keep doing things his own way. Only Mervin had a way to correct this – a whack on the side of the head, delivered at the most unexpected time and with utmost suddenness. It would stun Kabul for a moment, but after that he understood that enough is enough and he has to follow what Mervin said.

To my utter surprise, he meekly did so.

Both Mervin and Kabul were fond of flowering plants and we had a good garden. Mervin's contribution was limited to getting the plants, seeds and manure, and instructing Kabul on what was to be done. Kabul did all the planting and tending with great interest. Kabul believed that plants and flowers grew by talking and singing to them. Quite often we could hear him talking loudly to the plants and flowers.

Mervin had finally reconciled to Kabul acting on his belief and stopped saying anything. Still, whether to put fertiliser or not was an issue when it came to the garden. Kabul was not convinced that it was required. It was settled the normal way, with Mervin's unannounced whack.

The influence of Naxalism led Kabul to raise certain issues often. The most common one was on clothes. He would raise the issue almost every fortnight. " I have only three shirts but you have so many," he would start. "Everyone must have the same number of shirts," he would insist. "You should give some to me so that all of us have the same number."

The influence of Naxalism led Kabul to raise certain issues often. The most common one was his insistence that he should have the same number of clothes that we had. He would start the discussion by saying that he had only three shirts and while we had many more. He wanted us to give him or get him more so that he had as many as we did. Luckily he did not suggest that we destroy some of ours.

Luckily he did not suggest that we throw away some of ours. He was able to convey his views through a long monologue in his native language, with a lot of gestures thrown in. Kabul would have picked it up from the propaganda in his village.

In spite of the language barrier I could understand most of what he was trying to say while Mervin understood very little.

This used to happen in the evening after Kabul had served tea when we were back from the office. Mervin used to give him a patient hearing, kept looking back straight at him and at times made gestures as if he was sympathising with him. I felt that he did so sincerely.

To make Kabul feel better and less agitated, Mervin would explain to him as to why we needed more clothes. "We go to the office every day and meet many people. We have to be well dressed, with clean clothes. You stay at home, you do not need as many." At times Mervin's patience surprised me.

Yet there was no way to reach a conclusion to Kabul's satisfaction. Finally when it was dinner time, Mervin would signal to Kabul to come closer. There would again be a sudden whack, and Kabul would quietly go to the kitchen. All was normal again. To me the solution looked rather ancient and violent, but it worked.

With his Catholic background, Mervin was particular about honesty. Every Sunday he would take Kabul on his bike for weekly shopping, including vegetables. A list was made before they started. Kabul was supposed to remind him and make sure that all the items have been bought. Invariably while cross checking on return, Mervin would identify a couple of items that Kabul did not remind him about. "Oh! I picked them up," Kabul would say with extreme nonchalance.

Mostly this happened with items that were required in small quantities and common vegetables. Mervin was particular in selecting the best vegetables. While he did this for the green and seasonal vegetables, Kabul would quietly put items like coriander, ginger, green chillies, lemon and even some onions and potatoes in the bag. This angered Mervin no end. In spite of a lot of counselling and whacks, Kabul did not give up the habit. At last Mervin found a solution by giving some extra money to the vegetable vendor every week and absolve himself of the sin of turning a blind eye to stealing.

Kabul was otherwise quite honest and did his work slowly but meticulously. He would nicely lay out the food for us on the dining table and the quantity he made was such that enough was left for him after we had finished. He was happy on the food front as he ate the same food as we did. The only exception was when fish was there in the menu. Mervin brought a limited quantity and very often he would question Kabul on why so little was served. Kabul tried to convince us that all the fish had been brought to the table.

Sometimes Mervin would not give up. After asking him to get all the fish, with Kabul protesting that no more was there, he used to search the kitchen. Invariably some pieces were found hidden in different places each time. It practically became a game between the two. Kabul tried new ways and places to hide the pieces of fish, and Mervin would invariably find them. I could not fathom why he always hid the extra pieces only in the kitchen and nowhere else. In the end Kabul brought those pieces also to the table and Mervin gave him a whack, and the matter was settled for that day.

We gave Kabul two new sets of new clothes every year at Durga Puja time. In addition we used to keep giving him our used shirts and trousers. He could manage to use my shirts, Mervin's were too large for him. He had found a cheap tailor who altered our pants to his size, so he could use all the trousers we gave him. Over a year he built up a sizeable number, and his rants on equality in clothes practically ended. Yet he created new reasons all the time to get a whack from Mervin. It was almost as if he felt that it was Mervin's way of showing his concern and affection towards him.

Indians are often devoted to their masters

THE STRANGELY INTERESTING AND ANECDOTAL SAURABH SHUKLA

Bharti Sinha

Saurabh Shukla, SS for short, in his vague, inimitable style, entered my life with a bang – literally – when he walked straight into me with a glazed unseeing look, typical of only the most extreme cases of absentmindedness.

As I struggled to pick myself and my widely scattered belongings off the floor, all 5 foot 2 inches of SS stood eyeing me with a mildly quizzical look as he tried to decipher why a young lady would cast herself and her possessions at his feet!

Thus began my discovery of a being so alien to anyone I had ever known (or was ever to know since); and so unintentionally entertaining, that even a passage of over two decades since has failed to dim the memories of his hilarious, albeit unwitting, contribution to the joys of this world.

Shortly after we met in such a direct and dramatic fashion I was plunged, along with 15 other co-beneficiaries, into a residential in-house training program in a recently opened star hotel in the heart of the city for seven long weeks. One of the privileged 16 was also SS. However, "residential" was a novel concept for SS who, having always been a home bird, had never spent a single night in his 26 odd years away from his own home and hearth. (This, I learned from the horse's mouth, the horse in question being SS!)

Therefore, you can imagine what portents of doom and disaster this spelt for his mother who, it seems, was absolutely certain that some conniving, shrewish harridan was lying in wait ready to plunge her long, red-painted, perfectly manicured claws into her beloved son and heir and tear him away from the protective fold of his fond family. That the apple of her eye would follow temptation willingly and besotted, she did not doubt, the certainty brought on, no doubt, due to SS's penchant for the king of chocolate, Hindi film-like romance spinners in the '60s to '80s, Gulshan Nanda.

I can vouch for this first-hand, as I have personally seen his hoard of this precious literature stowed under lock and key, away from the prying and mischievous eyes of would-have-liked-to-bemarauders, in his office desk. SS would wind up work each day and then spend long hours each evening devouring each and every soulful syllable, away from the unending refrain of his mother's warnings to steer clear of evil temptation.

Possibly the delight of indulging in the romantic and sinful fantasies dangled by these books made him stretch the truth when he informed his mother of long work hours brought on by the pressures and work overloads. This was also the reason behind his glassy-eyed look and his besotted, wistful pout as he receded into a dream world, where, no doubt, he mouthed sweet nothings into the shell shaped ears of the doe- and dewy-eyed virginal heroine, yet to star in his parched world.

Well, to come back to his dilemma of how to straddle the problem of managing Mother and also attending the essential-for-career-continuity training, SS was able to extract a "parole-like" permit from his mother. This entailed his being permitted to carry at a time only one change of clothes, which necessitated his needing to report in person each evening at his home front, so that his Mom, under guise of supplying fresh change, also ensured he could not skip town.

You will by now have gauged how his sheltered and regimented existence had ensured that SS's innocence, despite his years, remained intact, shielded as it was from the sophisticated wicked ways of the world. SS remained therefore, almost childlike in his trust and belief and hence served up as prey to the predators who would shortly introduce him to experiences testing his gullibility and mental equilibrium!

His sheltered and regimented existence had ensured that SS's innocence, despite his years, remained intact, shielded as it was from the sophisticated wicked ways of the world. SS remained therefore, almost childlike in his trust and belief and hence served up as prey to the predators who would shortly introduce him to experiences testing his gullibility and mental equilibrium!

And his adventures started on his very first evening when he was introduced to his roommate, who convinced him to "volunteer" to take the bed towards the wall, take his turn in the bath last, to stand in the corridor while he changed, or speak to his girlfriend – sometimes forgetting to call him in after finishing, leaving SS shuffling sheepishly as passers-by gave him curious looks.

The same evening, the entire team gathered in the restaurant where a long table had been laid out in one corner for our group. SS, to his horror and distress, had been given a seat next to me – a "girl" – and thus a potential temptress. His furtive glances in my direction whenever he thought (wrongly) that I was looking elsewhere, alerted me to his fears and also, I am sorry to confess, tempted me to embark on a deliberate path to take unfair advantage of his innocence. Fate presented me with a chance as soon as dinner was over and finger bowls arrived. Probably, since SS had never seen a finger bowl in his life before, caution deserted him, as he looked left and right and then asked me "what" this "new dish" was!

I swear, I would not have made the first move, but presented with such an opening to provide the evening entertainment; I was only human and, lost to all hope, I gave my soul up to the devil as I answered, with a straight face and in a loud and carrying voice, "An after-dinner digestive drink".

Hearing my voice boom across the length of the table, 14 sets of fingers, poised and ready to plunge into the lemon-water, drew back as necks craned, and eyes strained looking out for the "What next"! Having got everyone's undivided attention, I went on, helpfully, shamelessly elaborating on the Emily Post way on the correct procedure to squeeze the lemon floating in the water, season with salt and pepper, holding the bowl correctly between both hands, craning the neck backwards at a 50 degree angle and finally tossing off the contents in one shot.

A keen and eager learner on social niceties and etiquette, SS obliged, stopping only once, since this was his first time, to correct the salt seasoning. Once done, he looked around the table with some curiosity wondering at the tardiness of the rest of the congregation sitting still. His eyes nearly fell out of his head, as he then watched 15 people, daintily dipping and washing fingers in the bowl, wiping these carefully on the white napkins, before meeting his stricken eyes and laughing uproariously!

You would have thought that having been bitten once, SS would have given his tormenter in chief, that is me, as well as those known cronies of mine, as wide a berth as possible. Alas for him, not being one of the world's leading minds, SS was drawn to us like a moth to the proverbial flame. This therefore provided all of us much merriment over the next seven weeks at his cost while we each tried to outdo each other as to how many times in a day we could make him fall into our trap. It was not really tough, I must admit as we only needed to give an opening and SS would walk straight into it, never suspecting us despite all the evidence to the contrary. This led to the next testing episode in his life.

He had just walked into the hotel reception one evening as a few of us were walking out for a stroll. It was evident from the paper package he was clutching that he had just returned from his daily trip home with his clothes for the night and following day. Seeing him walk in, we forced him to come out for a walk, asking him to hand his clothes package in at the reception. As soon as he stepped out, one of our party picked the package up and hid it inside a dustbin in the reception area, thinking that after he had conducted a heavy search we would produce it.

On our return, when he asked for the clothes, the receptionist told him, correctly, that someone had collected these immediately on his behalf stating that they would keep it in his room for him. As he made his way up to his room unsuspecting any foul play, we gleefully watched him for the next 2 hours go from room to room conducting thorough searches and inviting several uncomplimentary personal remarks for the missing clothes. Around 11 o'clock, we decided that the fun had been worthwhile and entertaining, but now with bedtime approaching we might as well put him out of his misery.

Hence an emissary was sent forth to retrieve the package. To our horror, nearly half an hour later he returned empty-handed. Sometime earlier the trash had been cleared and also collected by the garbage disposal. There was nothing left to do but to take the cowardly way out, and without admitting guilt, get one of our party to donate a pair of pyjamas to the suffering SS.

However, while SS did take the pyjamas, he spent the whole night as well as the next day searching for the permanently lost package. The final cut was when he refused to go home for two whole days, until, forced by the rich aroma being emitted by his un-fresh clothes, we admitted guilt and he went home. Of course his Mom did not believe him, fearing the worst, evidenced by his red face and swollen eyes, which he sported for at least a couple of weeks after that.

There were other interesting episodes over the years in my interactions with SS, tinged with humorous overtones, even if only from a single perspective. However, over the years, one came to see through the simpleton side of SS and came face to face with a heart of gold.

Before dropping further mention of SS, I would still like to unequivocally state that SS is probably the dream companion to see a "masala" Bollywood movie with. I still remember how a couple of us were making our way to see the late night show of Kumar Gaurav's "Love Story" in a theatre in Central Delhi, when we met SS in the doorway. Our polite and half-hearted invitation to him to join us was greeted with an instant and joyful agreement, leading us to immediately regret our foolhardiness. Never have I been so mistaken in my early impressions as I was that night.

The moment the credits started playing at the start of the movie we all realised that we were in for a rare treat as we saw SS leaning far forward in his seat, in dire danger of sliding out as he, with bated breath, shining eyes and eager anticipation concentrated on the 70mm CinemaScope screen. From that moment forward, all of us sat looking sideways at SS's face which registered in the fullest intensity every one of the "Navrases" being enacted on screen. The tragedy of young love being thwarted by parental obtuseness, the villainy threatening the very lives of the heroic couple, the comic relief that the buffoonery provided was all played out in truthful reflection on SS's face. His childish giggles interspersed with big, fat tears rolling down his plump cheeks, all served to give us more than our money's worth.

In fact, I understand after our recounting of the delightful experience, at least three sets of movie goers took him to see the same movie and, as per each report, the intensity of emotions displayed did not pall despite the frequency.

Today, on looking back, while I do regret that hard-heartedness of youth which made us all target SS to face the brunt of our cruel tricks and jokes, his innocence and lack of what would have been very justifiable anger has made me, in retrospect, hold SS in affectionate regard for his uncanny ability to trust and see good in others.

SS, if you read these pages, and understand them, do note that you are a world apart and I hope your simplicity remains shielded from the likes of us!

Naiveté of some Indians is hard to believe

KNOW THY NEIGHBOUR

Rajeev Lal

I was working in Madras (now Chennai) when I got married in 1975. Through a close friend in Delhi I was able to get on rent a one-bedroom apartment in a very good, quiet neighbourhood. It was part of a row of three-storey buildings. The apartment I got was on the top floor. It had a drawing cum dining room, a large bedroom, a kitchen, two bathrooms and a small balcony attached to the drawing room.

The owner was working in Delhi and was due to retire from service. He had furnished the flat completely in anticipation of occupying it soon. He got an extension for a year in his job, so he wanted to let it out for a year. This suited us very well – we did not have any furniture of our own at that time.

About ten days after we had moved in and settled down, we thought of getting to know some neighbours and making friends in the colony. The first initiative was with the people staying in the flat opposite ours. On a Sunday morning, I and my wife rang the doorbell of the flat. We had seen the nameplate "Rangachari" next to the door and had also seen an elderly person in his sixties a couple times coming out of the flat. He was dressed in immaculate white lungi and shirt on both the occasions and wore a tilak on his forehead prominently. He was slightly bald, had completely grey hair and wore spectacles.

Mr. Rangachari answered the bell and peeped out of the door. "Yes?", he craned his neck. "We have just moved in here. We wanted to meet our neighbours", I said. It seemed that he would allow us inside, but his gaze was at our feet. I read his thoughts – I had already spent three months in Madras and knew that footwear should be left outside the house. I quickly removed my shoes and kept them on the side of the door. My wife followed and kept her chappals next to mine. The door was opened for us to enter. "Come in Mr. Rajeev Lal", he said crisply as he read the new nameplate that I had put on my door.

Mr. Rangachari answered the bell and peeped out of the door. "Yes?", he craned his neck. "We have just moved in here. We wanted to meet our neighbours", I said. It seemed that he would allow us inside, but his gaze was at our feet. I read his thoughts – I had already spent three months in Madras and knew that footwear should be left outside the house.

The drawing room had a large straw mat with

coloured stripes laid against one wall. At the end near the balcony there was an old style large easy chair with extended hand rests. It had a woven cane seat and back and a thin cushion was placed on the seat. Mr. Rangachari waved us towards the mat and as we took our seats there; he occupied the easy chair. There was no other furniture in the room.

On the wall there was a calendar with the picture of lord Venkateswara and two large black and white photos in glass-covered frames. They were of an old couple, and sandalwood garlands had been put on both frames. We surmised that these were of Mr. Rangachari's deceased parents.

A middle-aged lady, stout and short, in her late forties entered the room. She wore a drak coloured sari with an attractive border. "Rukmini, meet Mr. and Mrs. Rajeev Lal. They live in the opposite flat", he told her. "This is my sister Rukmini", he quickly added to our benefit.

She gave us a curious look and went straight into the kitchen. She was back with two small steel tumblers with water and gave one to each, with a friendly smile. We weren't thirsty, but took the glasses and held them in our hands.

Rukmini sat down on the floor opposite to us. She seemed very pleased that someone had come to the house. We told them about us – where I worked, that we had got married just a month back, that we belonged to north India, etc. We learnt that Mr. Rangachari had recently retired from a private company after working there for over thirty years. They were well off but not rich, and Rukmini did not get married. Mr. Rangachari also did not marry due to this reason. They lived a peaceful life and did not have many friends and visitors. They were Brahmins and strict vegetarians.

"So what can I do for you Mr. Lal?", Mr. Rangachari asked me once these short introductions were over. " We just came to introduce ourselves as your next door neighbours and say hello", I said. Mr. Rangachari looked at me with a slight frown on his forehead. "We will try to meet some others also today", I said.

"How?" He seemed concerned. "will you ring their doorbells like you did here?" I realised that he was not amused with what we had done to him. "May be you can introduce us to the people downstairs", I suggested. "We do not know anyone in this building", he replied tersely and closed the subject.

By this time Rukmini was trying to make some conversation with my wife in broken English, and some Hindi words thrown in occasionally. In between she asked her brother to help by translating from Tamil what she wanted to say. We came to know that she was fond of Hindi movies and even went alone sometimes to watch them.

Rukmini asked my wife how good she was at cooking and offered to help if needed. "Many young girls these days do not know cooking, and that creates problems when they got married," she said. My wife just smiled and avoided mentioning the problems she too was facing on this account.

Mr. Rangachari seemed to be getting anxious about something in the meantime. At last he could not restrain himself. "Mr. Rajeev Lal, can you please tell me what work you have with me? I can't believe that you have come to meet me with no purpose", he said almost raising his voice. I understood the gravity of the situation.

My mind quickly raced to find a purpose of our visit, and luckily I found one. "Sir, I came to ask you where the nearest post office is". I quickly told him. That calmed him down a little, and he explained the location and the directions to the nearest post office enthusiastically. His face had the pride of sharing his knowledge that would be useful to us.

I got up just as he finished and pulled my wife's hand too, much to her surprise. I wanted to be out of the door before Mr. Rangachari had the slightest doubt that I had faked a purpose for our visit.

After the first experience of the morning, we did not have the courage to try and befriend any more neighbours that day.

Rukmini started coming to our home during

the daytime occasionally and found ways to communicate with my wife. But she never agreed to have a cup of tea or even a glass of water in our home. My wife felt that this was because we took non-vegetarian food also. One day when she came in, she found my wife talking to a young man seated in the drawing room.

"He is Mansoor," my wife introduced the visitor. " He has started a new service to collect orders from home and supply fresh vegetables." Such services were a novelty at that time. A few shopkeepers would arrange delivery at home.

"We do not allow Muslims in our house," Rukmini said after Mansoor left. My wife had been brought up in Lucknow, which has a mixed population with a large number of Muslims. Some of her good friends, and of her family, were Muslims. She found Rukmini's comment a little odd, but let it pass.

My mother and sister came to visit us after a month. All the ladies planned to see a new Hindi movie, and Rukmini was happy to join them. They had a good time. Rukmini was quite pleased; she could ask them to explain some dialogs that she couldn't understand.

At the end of the movie, they came out of the theatre in the evening. Across the road there was a line of a few small roadside restaurants. Rukmini suggested that they have snacks and tea. My wife was taken aback, not expecting that Rukmini would eat outside her own home. All of them followed Rukmini into the restaurant that she seemed familiar with.

Obviously, she had been there earlier. She ordered her favourite vegetable samosas and masala tea, which were quite good and everyone enjoyed these. As they came out, my wife saw the name board "Ashraf Hotel" which meant that the restaurant was owned by a Muslim. In the items listed at the bottom, she noticed mutton samosas and patties.

On returning home my wife told my mother and sister about her past conversations with Rukmini, and that she did not even accept a glass of water in our home. Recounting her enthusiasm to visit and eat at the restaurant which served non-vegetarian food too, they had a hearty laugh.

Some conservative Indians in a few states cannot fathom normal social interaction

MANAGEMENT GURU OF THE GOOD OLD DAYS

Rajeev Lal

An Indian operation of a global MNC in FMCG usually attracts top notch professionals and the crème-de-crème of the corporate world. This company was no exception and prided itself on also investing in state-of-the-art technology and widespread use of computers. I joined them at Calcutta (now Kolkata) in the early seventies.

The company had a massive information services department called EDP, short form for Electronic Data Processing in the old days. It was headed by a very polished gentleman, Mr. Jauhari, who had risen from the ranks starting as a Programmer.

He, however, at the point this narrative starts, seemed to have hit the glass ceiling. He was already designated General Manager. As he saw no scope for further promotions, he decided to opt for voluntary retirement with very lucrative benefits.

EDP managers were at the time a scarce commodity, and with the young Numero Deux in the department declining to move into the retiree manager's position, the company was thrown into a quandary. Consequently, although it was not made public, an open offer was extended for this position to all the senior managers in the company, with no takers.

The situation became further complicated, as there was also trouble in Paradise with the unionised staff members of the department becoming restive and spoiling for a fight. The advent of improved technology and more streamlined systems had reduced the need for people, and this had caused resentment with the impending threat of manpower reduction. While the reductions were taking place only in other departments and the EDP department was in fact growing in size, the staff in the department followed the diktat of the union on this issue too.

Finally, Mr. Varma, a brave man indeed, agreed to take up this fraught-with-challenge assignment. Mr. Varma, a veteran in the company, had already served in many functions across the company with the longest stint being in Finance. He knew the power of money better than anyone. To the EDP department team he was an unknown entity, and his coming was viewed with curiosity as well as a little trepidation.

Mr. Varma, contrary to all expectations, turned

out to be a very jolly and friendly soul. Every evening, around fifteen minutes past the office closing time, he would walk up to the table of one or the other officers in the department saying, " I need to discuss something important, let's go somewhere outside the office". The manner in which he asked brooked no argument, and the chosen officer would follow him meekly to one of Varma's popular favourite bars nearby.

Drinks would be ordered with Varma placing his own orders freely and frequently. As the clock struck nine, Varma, a stickler for punctuality it seems, would move swiftly to the next item on the agenda and order food – tandoori chicken, daal makhani, rumali roti and fish fry to be topped off with cassata ice cream – all ordered and polished off with the ease born of years of practice.

The crowning glory of the evening would be when, with loud burps of approval, he would permit the favoured host of the day to do the honours. In any case the host was supposed to present the damages for reimbursement at the end of the week when Mr. Varma would verify and approve this legitimate business expense!

These outings however, were merely harbingers of more good times to come. Official parties on Fridays were special occasions – started for the first time in the history of at least the EDP department – with the whole department including the unionised staff being invited to parties at the elite club in the city. For most of the people it was a once in a lifetime honour as they had no access otherwise to this select club! To the utter dismay of the Secretary of the Union, who happened to be from the EDP department, everyone who was part of the union also joined the parties in spite of a clear directive to the contrary. What else could one expect in a department where the average age of employees was twenty-six?

After a couple of such parties when disciplinary action was initiated against the Secretary, alas, none of his colleagues in the department stood up for him.

Many new changes were then implemented in the department and all were accepted with enthusiastic whoops over cheers and beers. The company had never seen such an effective and successful EDP Manager!

This was not the only area where Varma left his indelible mark. He also diligently reviewed each and every executive's work personally. He did the same for one of my reports. I sat in front of him in his cabin, with each one of us holding a copy of my report. I began in customary fashion by highlighting the salient features in each section. All through, Varma, with a beatific smile fixed on his face, kept nodding his head in a circular fashion.

On every page, he would encircle, in bright green

ink, some word or phrase. At the end of the review he would say, "looking good, see my markings!" Our department typist, Miss Lily, was exasperated at the number of iterations each report went through her to make the changes. In those days there were only typewriters, no word processors. After the third such review of the revised and re-typed report, I exchanged notes with my colleagues.

"Do you know he wears a hearing aid?" I replied in the affirmative as a colleague asked me. It transpired that Varma would switch off his hearing aid as soon as the review started and switch on his music system that had an earphone. That explained the copybook smile and rhythmic nodding of the head. The circles he drew on each page were meant to convey to his boss that he had gone through the report meticulously. Therefore the final version of the report also needed several green circles religiously strewn across.

It transpired that Varma would switch off his hearing aid as soon as the review started and switch on his music system that had an earphone. That explained the copybook smile and rhythmic nodding of the head.

The choice of colour probably owed its origin to his "auditing" past!

The way to exit this chakravyuh (maze) of reviews required an insistence that the report be forwarded upwards. He would then, with a disapproving frown on his face, look very seriously at the requester, take out a blue pen, and write "Forwarded for Approval". This was at variance from the practice followed by Mr. Jauhari, who used to write "Approved" or "Recommended for Approval". Varma wanted no share of responsibility for the actions of his subordinates. He did not know what they were trying to do, and had no interest in finding it out either.

We got used to taking a lot of initiative and doing things our way. Varma encouraged this in everyone as long as the person was loyal to him.

The grapevine revealed that the only condition that Varma had put to take up the unpopular assignment of EDP Manager was an unlimited expense account. He had his own ways of keeping his boss(es) happy. On one occasion, I happened to stay in the same hotel as our Director, his boss, was to check in. Around 8.30 a.m., while I was going out to the office, I saw Varma standing in the porch waiting for the boss to arrive. Tucked under each one of his arms was a full bottle of the boss's favourite scotch whiskey. How could any of his suggestions ever be turned down?

Varma, in his inimitable style, managed to succeed despite displaying none of the industry best practices imparted in the leading business schools the world over.

A year after he took over, he asked me to take over as head of the Electronic Data Processing (EDP) unit in Madras (now Chennai). I moved there and was spared of the frequent torturous evenings that I was forced to spend with him. I was not married at that time and so had been an easy target for frequent important discussions outside the office in the evenings. After a few times, even the free drink and delicious food could not lure me into spending a whole evening listening to his stories that had become repetitive, though he never realised it himself after a couple of pegs were inside him.

After six months, Varma decided to have a review at my location. Madras was a "dry" city – liquor was prohibited by law. So he had asked for the appropriate arrangements to be made. This involved the caretaker of the company guest house getting alcoholic drinks from the black market. For everyone's safety these were consumed in the guest house only. In addition to the internal review, Varma was to meet the EDP Manager of the company from which we used to hire computer time. Our company did not have its own mainframe computer installation at Madras.

The schedule for the evening on which he arrived at Madras was very tight. The EDP Manager Varma was to meet was a local person, very simple and religious, who used to finish his dinner latest by

7 p.m. This was the time Varma was scheduled to reach the guest house for his evening drinks. The guest EDP Manager, a complete teetotaller, could not be invited to join us at the guest house. It was therefore agreed that we would meet him over a cup of coffee at 8 p.m. at a hotel near the guest house.

Varma started his evening ritual in time, but was not able to finish it by 8 p.m. as there was quite some quantity left in the bottle of scotch. He could manage to finish it a little after 8.30, and we rushed for the meeting. Luckily I had asked a colleague of mine to be at the hotel, and he kept the guest EDP Manager amused till we arrived. Varma was quite drunk, and the look on the face of the guest made me feel that he would have reported us to the police but for the fact that we were his main customers.

After the two were introduced, Varma did not give the guest a chance to open his mouth. He suddenly started narrating the highlights of the flush (Indian poker) cards game he had with his friends the previous night with great gusto. "He played blind – I also played blind", he started. "He played blind – I also played blind", he repeated thrice. The guest's mouth was wide open. Tolerating a drunkard itself was too much for him; a gambler on top of it? He wanted to get up and run, but Varma did not even pause to give him time to say or do anything.

In between I tried to interrupt and raise the issue of reduced computer rental, which was our objective for the meeting but Varma gestured me to keep quiet. The guest started yawning after twenty minutes, and we realised that things could take and ugly turn if the meeting was not ended soon. Finally a few minutes before 9.30 p.m., I and my colleague got up from our chairs, literally pulled Varma out of his, made him shake hand with the guest and my colleague escorted the guest out. I followed a few steps behind with Varma.

I got the feeling that the guest EDP Manager looked happy and relieved as he left. After all the subject of computer rental that we wanted to discuss never came up. Instead of being upset, he may have wished for more Varmas in our company.

I had been married in the meantime, and the last event for the day was to pick up my wife from home and then go to the best 5-star hotel in town for dinner. Varma had said that he wanted to do this. I had told my wife that we would reach home around 8:45 p.m. – we were over an hour late. There were no cell phones at that time, and we did not have a phone at home either.

In her enthusiasm, my wife had made some light snacks to welcome Varma and re-heated them twice expecting our arrival. She was red-faced and angry as she opened the door. There was no way to have the snacks, and this added to her rage. I still persuaded her to leave the eats on the table as they were and come with us for dinner. The excitement that she had in the morning for dinner in a restaurant which we could not afford to visit on our own had completely vanished.

Most of the guests at the posh restaurant were already leaving by the time we entered it, and the steward and waiters looked at us with trepidation writ on their faces. I reminded the steward of our reservation which was for about an hour and a half earlier. He nodded and brought the menu. Three waiters huddled in a corner looked at him and then at our table, concerned about the likely extended shift. Varma studied the menu carefully – he was never in a hurry.

He almost jumped from his seat when he saw "Lobster Thermidor" in the menu. He looked at the steward and told him his main choice, pointing it out in the menu with his finger. The steward craned his neck, read the item and winced.

"Sir, this will take at least forty five minutes to prepare", he said. "We are in no hurry", said Varma and ignoring the stewards mild protestation, went ahead to order the rest of the items. For the next half an hour, over the soup and starters, Varma described the heavenly experience he had eating Lobster Thermidor during one of his recent visits overseas and how he had been looking forward to finding it in the menu in India ever since.

It was 11 p.m. by the time the main course came

to the table. The Lobster Thermidor was served with the shell and fins as part of the decoration on the plate. My wife did not like the sight of it and did not take any. It was delicious, and after I took a small helping, Varma monopolised the Thermidor and finished it completely. We took about half an hour to finish the main course and leave the restaurant. We reached home past midnight. My wife did not speak to me for two days, luckily including the day that had already started as we entered our home. Only after my stupendous effort to consume all the snacks that she had prepared (some of them toughened by being reheated multiple times) in those two days, did she start speaking to me again.

In three years Mukherjee, the officer who had refused to take over as manager got so frustrated and fed up of the continuous persuasion by all of us to do something, that he offered to become the EDP Manager. Varma was promoted and given back his role in the Finance Dept. The importance of the role can be judged by the fact that there was no appointment in between for that role in Varma's absence.

The junior staff gave him a tearful farewell. He had endeared himself to the team. The tears though were more for the likelihood of the great parties coming to an end with his departure. It happened so. The EDP Department was never the same again. There was marked improvement in the efficiency and sense of direction in the department. The expenses came down significantly, which was appreciated by the top management. Still people remembered with nostalgia the fun, frolic and freedom we had enjoyed under Mr. Varma. I was no exception.

Indians are malleable, and will return favours

OF ROMEOS, LOTHARIOS AND PINING HEARTS!

Bharti Sinha

The entry into any male bastion of a winsome, easy-on-the-eye, budding Helen of Troy look-alike, can instantly catapult an erstwhile club of bonhomie-and-camaraderie into a testosterone over-laden hotpot where circling-while-eyeing-each-other with mistrust and suspicion becomes the order of the day.

This is even more acute in high technology companies. Used to being toasted and much sought-after, (evidenced by the mind-boggling rates being bandied about in the matrimonial marketplace), these specimens of corporate cream suddenly find the fiend within waking up and urging them with passionate prods to act rather than work on drawing up a long-term strategy, since time is of the essence.

Jostling shoulders and stamping toes, these huffing, puffing, red-faced, glazed-eyes souls quickly shrug off all the carefully nurtured and well-practised manners that their B-schools have, in true Harvard-inspired fashion, drummed into these stars.

With hormones raging, caution is thrown to the winds, while they each try to outdo one another as they promise weekend treats, daily drops home each evening, and also, from the more desperate one, a morning pickup as well.

Just a few days before, sipping cocktails and discussing the latest industry predictions by global stalwarts, one would not have expected even an earthquake less than 7.0 on the Richter scale to ruffle one hair on their Brylcreem-doused heads, or raise one well-shaped eyebrow on their facial-pampered, carefully controlled faces.

Sipping cocktails and discussing the latest industry predictions by global stalwarts, one would not have expected even an earthquake less than 7.0 on the Richter scale to ruffle hair on their Brylcreem-doused heads, nor raise one well-shaped eyebrow on their facial-pampered, carefully controlled faces.

The moment however, a dimpled damsel enters their lives, the same denizens of civilised life can easily be mistaken as lovelorn romancers of old, with their Viking instincts ruling paramount as they ready themselves to duel unto death for the fair lady's attentions.

The heroine meanwhile, is taken aside by the

proactive hero with first-mover advantage, who having spotted her Daddy drop her at the gate, is already planning long drives with her in his new, leased car, wondering how long before he will be required to invest in dark film on his car windows, while he explores the hidden delights of life's first love when one has money in the bank!

No matter how foolhardy and lost, however, there are some initial basics of etiquette which must be gone through before crossing the point-of-no-return – viz. Is she married, engaged or dating? Has she any brothers, and if so, their age and physical dimensions? What does Daddy do or can do? Is he in the police, or mafia or income tax? Such are the all-important life-and-death preliminary queries.

Having once ascertained "All Is Well" as espoused by Bollywood's 3 Idiots, he proceeds to coo in her delicate ears, promising many treats, if only she would be willing to start with, go home a little later – he would of course see her home "safely" as he "had a car, you see"!

A few such "safe trips" where the only contact were the occasional "accidental" brushes of his hand against her hand or knee, (while changing gears), are a necessary next step, while the young, polished techie, with a promising career, sets her fears at rest.

Soon, encouraged by his obvious, protective

interest in her, she finds herself baring her young soul, its heartaches, family problems, her first kiss ,(yet to come or already happened), with this platonic, almost brother-like colleague, so much nicer than the others – panting bevy of guys – who seem to do little else other than ogling her with bullfrog eyes!

A week or two or this and then our hero is ready with his next move. After dropping her home one evening he will suddenly reappear at her door, armed with a dainty, lacy handkerchief, or book or some other prop, which he believes she may have left behind in his car.

"Namaste Auntie-ji", (for it is she who answers the doorbell), "So sorry to disturb and all that, but Isha, your daughter; (such a bright, intelligent and well brought up girl – already doing so well – will certainly go places says Boss); seems to have left this in my car. Don't know if she can wait till tomorrow or not so I came back to give it – no, no, no bother at all.

No one waiting at home na, Mummy-ji and Papa-ji are at Papa-ji's posting you see. Food? I will go back and cook something – rice and daal (lentils) and some achaar (pickle) Mummy made for me. No trouble Auntie-ji, roz ki aadat hai (am used to this). After all bahar ka khana (outside food) is not good daily, no? But I miss Mummy-ji's cooking, after all ghar ke khane ka jawab nahin (there is nothing better than home-made food)!"

This, accompanied by a wistful, boyish pout, designed to tug at Auntie-ji's soft maternal heartstrings, succeeds in extracting a dinner invite – "Well, if you insist, and it's no trouble, mind you – but no formality Auntie-ji – just ghar ka khana".

Having thus infiltrated into the fortress that is an Indian "marriageable" girl's home and landed himself on the most well-guarded citadel – the dining table – the hero then focuses on entrenching himself as an on-his-way to becoming a fixture in the girl's home.

Starting by paying flattering attention to Uncle-ji's boring and unending tirade on the desh-ke-netas (country's leaders) who are responsible for the barbadi (ruination) and the spiralling costs, he proceeds to cement his firm foothold as he discusses recipes and predicts the what-next in the latest TV soap operas, pets and scratches Puppy-ji or Doggie-ji. Last, but certainly not the least, if any siblings are present, is making rash promises of maths or cricket lessons, or, in case the kid is a girl, acquiring autographs of Shah Rukh Khan, Shahid Khan or any other currently raging heartthrob.

By now, the whole office is agog to know the progress and where the hero-to-some-but-villain-to-them has reached in his insidious and vile designs.

With now the whole gang of would-love-to-have-been Romeos to this Juliet, uniting against this Lothario – common enemy and epitome of indecency – they start plotting to de-fang this snake-in-the-grass, this pretender to the throne around whom no virtuous girl is safe. Thus starts a parallel whisper campaign – "For your own good, you know...this rascal will now try to entice you into going out alone with him – for a long drive, you know – and then fake car trouble so you are forced to spend a night together...be very careful as these bachelor types coming into the city have no reputations and hence nothing to lose!"

Having bought time, they now target Boss, who is also suitably instigated by these frustrated upholders of corporate virtue, as they lament, "Is ladki ne yahan ka atmosphere bigad diya hai, (this girl has spoiled the atmosphere here),Sir – Ek to chakachak bolti hai, (for one she chatters non-stop) – so we can't concentrate, phir roz ise lift chahiye, jiski vajah se (and then she wants a ride home every day because of which) we can't work late...and have you noticed, Sir? Our hero is already entangled in her trap – Sir, please do something drastic and save him – transfer kar dijiye Sir – to a small, far flung location since he needs rest, he is a mental wreck and does not have the slightest inkling of what she is setting him up for!"

One day, however, our heroine comes traipsing in, laddoo-ka-dabba (box of sweets) in hand, and a shining solitaire diamond ring on her left hand, "De Beers, you know", as she prattles on about her engagement, just last evening, to her US-posted, H-1B Visa-enabled; "with green card sponsorship round the corner" IT Software whiz-kid fiancé. "Dus din mein shaadi hai (*wedding is in ten days*) – you all must come, haan?"

Ten days ensue and then peace prevails, the old

bonhomie restored, until the whiff of an expensive perfume, a few days later, stokes up the old raging fires and once again the free-for-all begins!

MARRYING OFF BOSS

Bharti Sinha

The box of sweets approached me slowly as it completed its circuitous route across the huge hall, populated by a neatly suited and tied or sari clad multitude doing their bit to boost the stock of the IT firm which doled out the monthly pittance, ambitiously called "salary".

As the grinning peon brought the "pedas", (a common sweet normally distributed to celebrate special occasions), to me, I wondered aloud who could be the one spreading largesse on a weekday, and that too, at the end of the financial quarter. "Koi order aya hai kya (Has someone won an order)?", I queried. "No-no, Saab (Sir) is distributing sweets" – incredulous and doubting that our famously miserly "boss" could be forking out from his hoarded wealth, he went on to clarify – "shaadi kar rahe hain (he is getting married)" – spreading light on a mystery that had threatened to fox us till the cows came home.

"What? When?", I asked. By now a small crowd of munching, chomping colleagues was thronging

– all equally dumbstruck by the prospect of there actually existing a girl who would agree to martyr herself to a lifetime with boss, with whom, as we knew first hand, even a half-day monthly review had us muttering unprintable curses and teetering on the verge of throwing our resignations. All except "Soapy" – so named because of his constant "soft-soaping" as he carried daily updates of our misdemeanours, real or imagined, to Boss!

Realizing no more intelligence was forthcoming from the lowly peon, we all turned to Soapy, who true to expectations, waxed eloquently as he found himself, for once, the undisputed centre or attention.

He revealed how he had been summoned last Sunday in the wee hours and had accompanied Boss and family to Karnal where the girl and her family lived and where the now famous engagement had taken place. His tale took on a visual body as he mesmerised us with a blow-by-blow run down on the events of the fateful day.

It seems all family members were given a solid 22ct. 1 gm. gold coin in "bidai (farewell)" by the girl's parents, and the "boy" – and unlikely term for the big bully who was Boss – was given a diamond ring, thick gold chain and bracelet, a Rolex gold watch – (the real thing, not the famous "Chinese" variety) – and Rs. 2,51,000 in cash for "shagun" (good luck). Needless to add that his Armani tie, suit, socks as well as Gucci shoes were also brought for him all the way from Italy by the girl's businessman brother. (Soapy could not satisfy one curious member of the audience on the make and colour of Boss's unmentionables – guess he wore his own!)

Eyes popped as we digested this news of a family actually blind to what was glaring to all of us – that Boss, while possibly not an eyesore, was certainly one of those creatures who crawl out in the dead of night from under a rock.

Soapy, meanwhile, went on with his tale of the momentous occasion – seems he too was bade farewell with a gold coin, but Boss took it away saying that it did not look good since Soapy, while "really close" was not "truly family", promising, as he did so, to return the same to the bride-to-be's family at a suitable moment in the distant future.

Marvelling at this bolt from the blue, all of us trooped into Boss's den to offer our felicitations and, to offer insincerely our services, should he need any help.

"Glad you offered", he simpered, as he proceeded to unblushingly hand each one of us a neatly printed list of action items each of us was expected to undertake. "All I could jot down just now – am sure there will be lots more as time gets on!"

I reeled as I saw 32 main items (if I didn't count the countless sub-items), all listed on five sheets of A4 sized pages, in Times New Roman font – size 10!

"I am specially counting on you" I heard him say as through a daze I realised that his object of address was me, "since you travel and are also, ahem, a lady" he went on, smirking.

"When"? I stammered. "The happy day is three months away – enough time"! Enough time for what – Loading the list? Driving us up the wall? Constant reviews now on the personal front in addition to work? Goofing up? The horror of our predicament caused the whole lot of us to start shaking uncontrollably like a particularly unstable jelly.

"Am off for the day but thanks for offering to help – am counting on you guys!", he prattled before he was off, leaving behind shell-shocked, witless victims – all struck by a common calamity!

Work was forgotten as we all trooped to the neighbourhood café to collect our wits and come to terms with the testing times that lay ahead.

I went from list to list, as I checked to see what others had been selected to do. No one was spared, as all had strenuous and time-consuming chores. The choicest, however, designed to test one on both objective as well as subjective levels, were reserved for me. Deviously disguised pitfalls lurked in plenty between yawning gaps, each threatening to engulf me, and with a sense of portending doom, I saw them there on a platter as though challenging me saying, "Ok, try this and see if you can pull a Houdini to extract yourself here".

The "heavy stuff" meted out to others was simpler to execute. Though none were spared as far as quantity of work went, most of those required mere outsourcing and coordination, such as organizing transportation for pickups, tents and marquees, sweets and savouries, etc.

My fare had stuff like – saris for the bride and Boss's close relatives, to be sourced from all over India – "You have such good taste so you choose – am sure it will be right" – an act not likely to go down too well with the bevy of female relatives in his household, all of whom would have their own individual ideas of what "tasteful" connoted, and all of whom, armed with the artillery of being Boss's Mom, or Sis etc. would not shy from bringing down their collective weights on my head.

I could almost hear the cacophony doing the rounds in my head. "Wonder what Munnoo (the unlikely pet name one had learnt sabre-rattling, teeth-gnashing Attila was called by those he had no power over) sees in her – he can't even recognise the correct shade of fuchsia when expressly asked to – did you see the sari for the mooh-dikhai (first look at the bride)? Positively pink, no?" And to think this was only one colour in one dress for one occasion out of somewhere in the vicinity of a million permutation-combination options!

Then matching blouse, bangles, fake imitation jewellery that looked real, and countless accessories – matching what? The border or base colour? Jewellery – gold, silver, diamond? Bangle size – 2.1, 2.25, 2.5? I shuddered at the prospect of falling flat many a time over answerable to not only one boss but to many super-bosses with no visible hope of success. As I looked around, I saw several surreptitious, pitying glances my way, reinforcing my worst fears as I looked towards the next few months with dread.

Hardening both my heart and my resolve, I realised that in order to live to tell the tale, I first of all needed a plan – both for the executions as well as to get the "delivery" accepted.

With no time to lose, I quickly retreated to the office to chalk up the action plan. I decided on a two-pronged approach:

- Prong one – Know *what* to do, and

- Prong two – Know *the enemy* – i.e. the entire Boss clan.

With no time to lose, I quickly retreated to the office to chalk up the action plan.
I decided on a two-pronged approach:
- Prong one – Know what to do, and
- Prong two – Know the enemy – i.e. the entire Boss clan.

I started with another look at the long list of action items that I grouped by location for sourcing. I then proceeded to compare and align these groups with my travel schedules. I then prioritised these on considerations, aligning the importance of the to-do item with the importance of clients in that location. For instance, sindoor (vermilion), ivory bangle, Tussar and Kantha saris and embroidered petticoats entailed a trip to Kolkata. Had I any customers there? Realizing there were few and all were stricken with the Hamlet syndrome, I decided that would have to enjoy a low priority, with Delhi's very own CR Park providing a backup option.

I knew, sadly, that not meeting the annual target was not an option!

The so-essential-to-a Hindu-bride Benaresi sari posed another predicament. The only time people were known to travel to Benares (or Varanasi as it was now known) was either to bid their dear departed final farewells or as mortal remains of themselves.

I knew then, that my next tour to the relatively business-friendly Lucknow needed to coincide with a weekend to enable me to make an expensive trip in a hired car to Varanasi. How I would justify a flight back from Varanasi to Delhi was a poser I had yet to work out – after all it was not likely that Boss's wedding was a justification that would go down well with the auditors (God knows why, though. Surely they too have bosses, don't they)?

By now my head was dizzy as the bleak future swam before my eyes – one long, unending serial disaster trail waiting to be blazed!

The next few days blurred by – with the occasional wails, groans and "blast hims" being the only sounds piercing through the unpartisan and omnipresent gloom that had descended on this congregation of an otherwise fairly light-hearted gang. Each one us realised that in this one venture we were on our very own – with consequences of failure promising certain and swift exits from the fold of this one company willing to keep us in, if not exactly gravy, at least bread and the occasional jam.

Realizing that the odds favoured failure, I took the precautionary first step of updating my CV and also renewed by contacts in the rival companies as well as the placement fraternity.

I then proceeded to step two of my action plan – requirement gathering and understanding – and, although here I harboured few hopes, setting expectations.

Hence, through the besotted (more likely by the glitter of the dowry than the charms of the hapless bride-to-be) boss, I obtained the invite to his lair to meet Boss's womenfolk!

I learned that this consisted of the grandé dame, Dadiji, (grandmother – a bearded lady with the Ancient Mariner look); Mummyji, (the one who was responsible for inflicting this top-notch source of our many woes on the unsuspecting world); Bhabhiji, (the elder brother's wife – who was now preening at the prospect of being promoted to "Jethaniji" or older daughter-in-law and hence to be obeyed and bowed to by the new entrant – second-in-command in the pecking order only to Mummyji, who as mother-in-law was Supremo). The other two ladies of influence who brought up the rear of this formidable kitchen cabinet, were Didi, (the much-married older sister), of the constipated expression, as if ready with pre-emptive disapproval no matter what, and Munni, the spoilt brat and precocious teenager, getting her first taste of being able to kick one around who could not bite back – i.e. yours truly!

As I crossed the threshold into boss's home bat the preordained time the following Sunday afternoon – (virtuously chosen since "we can't waste office time for personal work now, can we?") – I could hear Dadiji on being informed in response to her querulous "Kaun hai? Dopahar ko sone bhi nahin deta!" ("Who is it who has come to disturb our afternoon siesta?"). "The girl from Munnoo's office", bellowed Mummyji, "you know, the dark, short girl who is supposed to get all our clothes and tailoring done".

I was shown into a darkened hall to await Mummyji or some other denizen to arrive and kick off my sorry plight. Fifteen agonizing minutes later the entire battalion arrived, led by Dadiji, brandishing a fierce looking stick and an expression to match.

"You won't have any tea, will you?", asked Mummyji, carrying without waiting for a reply, "Bad for health you know, so soon after lunch".

Dismayed as I was at this very first indication that the battle lines were drawn, nonetheless, I proceeded to organize the entire project, akin to how I would at work.

I had come armed with the results of some homework ahead of this visit and hence, had:

- All functions listed
- All women in boss's clan listed
- Dates and Schedules
- Props such as a box of paints, paper, markers, pencil, staples and stapler, glue-stick, skeins of multi-coloured threads, etc. (These last were crucial since this was the only way I could pin people to the exact shades and colours they wanted – no way was I willing to get lost in the fuchsia or "particular purple" route).

Sensitive to protocol, I decided to start with Dadiji

(grandmother), and in no time was educated on the seven different shades of "white" – to which the added complexity of choice of material, (crepe, chiffon, muslin, silk and georgettes), borders – zari (gold, silver – dull or shining, bronze or copper – "antique") and self (that is woven in same shade) had me reeling.

Then followed Mummyji – green for mehndi, mustard for haldi (turmeric) – no make that yellow, "you know, the colour the sunflower is when seen under a cloudy sky, not the one bright and eye catching under the afternoon sun on a blue-sky day", pink for the shaadi, red for the mata-ki-chowki next day after the "bahu" (daughter-in-law) comes home and turquoise blue for the reception.

The above took up a good three hours – and I indulge in a bit of self-congratulation in having the good sense to come prepared, for I now have a paper with the right hues painted as well as swatches of coloured threads, and so, all but taking their thumbprints, I have ensured that they cannot now retract!

And now comes the tricky part – what is the budget? "You know, you can spend X" they advise – looking like they have generously given me carte blanche, while quoting an amount I know to be possibly ranging between 20%–25% of what the going price is.

"Auntie-ji", I stammer, "forgive me but the prices are around X+300%!" "No, no, you need to haggle", I am informed. "Don't you pay a paisa more, ok?"

It is not ok at all but I retreat in a cowardly fashion and then set up the next appointment for coming Saturday to capture Didi, Bhabhiji (sister-in-law) and Munni's wish list.

Come Monday morning and I wend my way to Munnoo's lair to elicit the spend money. "Use your credit card", I am informed, "I will pay you when the bill comes". "But Sir", I stammer, "the wholesale markets work on cash – and they are the only ones who allow you to negotiate". Trapped in the face of this unarguable fact, he reluctantly loosens the purse strings, issuing veiled threats should I be tempted to be generous with his fortune.

Thus armed, I embark on the execution of the plan, starting with my first trip to Mumbai – where I quickly manage to run through Dadiji's list. Of course I am greatly aided by beginner's luck as I discover that one of my customer's has a cousin who has a flourishing wholesale textile business and who also imparts generous discounts. Of course this is still double the budget I was allocated, so it is unlikely that I will get any brownie points for my efforts!

My return to Delhi armed with an order as well as the first leg of my shopping completed, I am rewarded with the proverbial pat on the back by boss and dark looks for my colleagues who have yet to show any progress and to whom I am now held out as evidence that they are "lazy laggards!"

Mummyji also, surprisingly, poses less problems since her tastes are garish and gaudy – styled after the fashion popularised by the heroines in time-honoured Punjabi films way back in the '60s and for which just one trip to Chandni Chowk and Karol Bagh suffices.

Puffed with pride, I report at the boss threshold, carting all the shimmering material and saris, and, accompanied by a darzi (tailor) who owed me since I had introduced him to a garment exporter friend, thereby setting him up in business a few years ago.

At least I could now sit back, sipping a coke as I watched Dadiji and Mummyji holding their breaths in, just so their waists and ample bosoms could be pulled in a couple of impossible inches, while the tailor, with a deadpan expression, took down their embarrassing vital statistics.

However, it soon transpired that this initial success was a mere flash in the pan, and I now found myself plunging into a deep abyss as the "Trio", not unlike Macbeth's three witches, started outlining their expectations. Not for them just the clothes, they also wanted accessories – shoes, bangles, jewellery, handbags, the perfect makeup, hair style, beauty treatment – in short the works!

Brat, alias Munni, actually went so far as to demand that she accompany me while I went shopping, in Delhi at least.

Resigning myself to the fact that several personal days and weekends were slated to vanish, I promised to call her after returning from my next leg of travel to both the hinterlands of India, as well as to Singapore – that Mecca for shoppers of all budgets!

For Bhabhiji, now nudging forty, I had to be the miracle-worker – to make sure that she outshone (literally in dazzling sequin-endowed finery) all, including the bride. I struck gold in Laad Bazaar, the famed street at Charminar in Hyderabad, where not only did I get the zardozi (gold and silver thread) embroidered and stone encrusted saris and lehnga-choli (long skirt-blouse)finery, but also the meenakari and "laakh" (wax lacquered) bangles to match. (The correct size was ensured due to my quick-thinking as I had taken the precautionary measure of bringing samples bangles of all the ladies). I also managed to extract good discounts on the famous pearl sets from the neighbouring Pathergatti, styles copied from famous designer-sets of just a few months' vintage, and at half the price.

In parallel, I was also posed a grave challenge – shopping for Didi – for not only did she need to outshine the bride, she also had to drip money, (without it actually needing to be spent), and nudge ahead of her arch rival – Bhabhiji. The fact that she was pear-shaped, (in contrast to Bhabhiji's almost anorexic Twiggy-like figure) meant that all the heavy embroidered and thick material was, I feared, likely to render her a tent-like appearance. I therefore resolved to source her stuff from Lucknow and Jaipur, sticking to delicate and lighter fabrics with finer embroidery, zardozi and weaves. Even her jewellery was to be one-gram gold sets famous in Rajasthan, with semi-precious stones.

The only poser was, how to convince both Bhabhiji and Didi that the stuff chosen for them was exactly their dream choice and not mine! This is where "Soapy", my trusty spy, proved his mettle as I, through guile and bribery, managed to elicit the necessary dope on who was the favourite reel-idol for each of them.

Learning that Katrina Kaif was Bhabhiji's ideal and Didi fancied the size-zero Bebo (or Kareena Kapoor), I put Photoshop to good use on the trusty laptop – thanking Bill Gates, Steve Jobs and the entire galaxy of computer gods from the bottom of my heart – morphing photographs of the selected saris, material and jewellery on to these actresses so that each could be shown what they would look like in their imaginations.

Armed with all these, I reported once again, a mere two weekends later, at the Boss household, earning not only a coke this time, but also samosas!

Now, all that remained in the apparel department were the dresses for pipsqueak and the bride, before I was free to move to the next steps – "imported stuff shopping", arranging the beauty parlour and spa, mehndi, sangeet and so on.

I selected the following Saturday and asked Munni to be ready to spend the whole day shopping with me. Having by now noted that she harkened to look trendy yet traditional, while at the same time also putting on at least five years, I decided to identify, ahead of the day, a few designer copy specialists, choosing Ritu Kumar and Sabyasachi inspirations.

Since one of the most critical ingredients, when you are seventeen, to being a grown up is the freedom to show cleavage and bare to dare the back and navel, I decided to start her off with the essential precursor – that is lingerie shopping! Helping her select sexy underwired lacy bras with invisible straps, and bikini panties which could peep through the flimsy material of her clothes and blouses, I could see from her ever-widening eyes that this was a new voyage of discovery for her. Never before had she realised that she too could have "breasts" which now propped appropriately, would allow her to give tantalizing glimpses to some of the "hot" boys she had spotted in the bride's camp during the engagement and who had not even spared her a fleeting glance.

We then made our way to the fake "designers" store and selected stuff in diaphanous and filmy material – all of which would have graced many a screen goddess in a Karan Johar movie. We followed this with slipper and sandal shopping – with a happy couple of hours being spent in her practicing walking and dancing, shod in silver, gold, copper, black and cream delicate sandals – all with slim 4 inch high stilettoes.

By now Munni had me firmly entrenched in her heart! My stock with her rose to an all-time high when we entered a cosmetics shop, and the shop assistant demonstrated how she could magically transform, with the use of make-up, her piggy-eyed and pimply faced look, to a flawless clear-skinned wide open eyed beauty.

That evening when we staggered back, armed with bags of shopping, the family urged me to stay on for dinner. Next evening I flew to Singapore, returning a week later with purses of all shapes, sizes, material and colours, perfumes, cosmetics for the bride as well as the ladies of the Munnoo clan, and a watch for the bride and groom!

I then proceeded, with lightning speed to wrap up the mehndi party, the bhajan singers for mata-ki-chowki, the beautician who, along with her army of assistants would tend to then transformational needs of the entire female troupe "at home", the beauty salon for the bride's makeup for the reception, and even a full time press-wallah to iron everyone's clothes.

Now only one thing that remained, and which was of course also the most critical – the bride's stuff. I decided to again start with a list:

- Saris (7 needed to be sent +1 for Reception) and a red-and-gold Lehnga
- Sindoor (vermilion powder and the mark of a married Hindu)
- Chunari (long scarf)
- Matching bangles and jewellery

The first thing I worked on was the lehnga (long skirt) – for which I scoured the entire Chandni Chowk and Karol Bagh markets. The instructions on this item were crisp and clear – "blood-red only" – I had been told, since this was "shubh (auspicious)".

Aware that this was universally considered the most auspicious choice, I was unprepared for how arduous and elusive this task would prove to be. I found pink and maroon, peach and purple, blue and turquoise, green and mustard, teal and fuchsia, but no reds! "No longer fashionable ji", I heard as a constant refrain. Finally when I was about to despair, I ran down the one specimen (probably in the whole of Delhi) in Karol Bagh. Luck was with me as this proved to be exquisite – satisfying both on extent of gold-work as well as on the finesse in workmanship. And I also managed to get it at a whopping discount of 50% –

"No one wants red these days, madam".

The rest of it was a breeze – I got a Pochampalli from Hyderabad, a Kanjeevaram from Chennai, a Paithani from Pune, a Banarasi from Varanasi, a traditional white, red and gold sari from Kolkota, a Bandhini and Chunari from Jaipur and a lehnga in crepe silk and chiffon from also Jaipur. The pièce de résistance however, was a rich Tanchoi, again from Varanasi for the reception.

Having now acquitted myself and having completed all the work in a record two months from start to finish – a whole month short of the D-day – I was also able to focus on justifying my existence by booking a record number of orders – all the visits I had to make for shopping yielding dividends. I was also now a welcome fixture in the Munnoo household, no longer an interloper. Instead, I was addressed as "beti" (daughter) or by name, as I scurried back and forth, smoothening any last minute glitches.

I was able, to as a bonus, also look down my supercilious nose at my hapless colleagues, who instead of getting down to it, had spent the entire duration in collectively griping and drowning their sorrows in the evening tipple, leading to the inevitable disasters and earning the daily ire of boss.

And finally, the icing on my happiness came when Boss, one day before proceeding on leave, was promoted and filled in his boss's shoes as he too got kicked upstairs and overseas. Inevitably, based on my stupendous and unchallenged performance, I am now Boss – hated and cursed by the multitude outside the spacious cabin I now occupy. And "Soapy" is now my male version of Mata Hari as he slithers in and out, bringing me the dirt on all.

I'm now wondering how to get another unmarried boss so I am assured of my next promotion!

Indian weddings are elaborate,
events to remember

ALWAYS RIGHT

Rajeev Lal

Navalkar was one of the most popular persons in the IT department. He was known for his quick wit, which saved many a situation, and as the trusted astrologer who always predicted correctly whether the forthcoming addition to one's family would be a boy or a girl. These two traits were good enough for him to assume that he need not strain himself by trying to do any work in the team. Luckily for him his assumption seemed to be right.

Navalkar was one of the most popular persons in the department. He was known for his quick wit, which saved many a situation, and as the trusted astrologer who always predicted correctly whether the forthcoming addition to one's family would be a boy or a girl.
These two traits were good enough for him to assume that he need not strain himself by trying to do any work in the team.

The Director in charge of the department was a very powerful executive. He had studied and lived in the UK, had impeccable style and manners.

He was well known for a temper that made him resemble a blast furnace when he lost it. Anything short of perfect was unacceptable to him. It was not uncommon for people to start trembling at the mention of his name, and one can imagine the terror his presence could create.

One day Doshi, Navalkar's boss, called everyone who mattered in the department to announce that the Director will be spending half a day in the following week to inspect the department and review its functioning. He looked terrified, as this was the first visit of the Director to the department after Doshi was promoted to head it. He started doling out tasks to everyone, yelling out of nervousness at anyone who disturbed his stream of thoughts with too many questions.

The tasks started from cleaning of the complete office, right to the drawers in the tables and all shelves and cabinets. The Director had on one occasion found the place that he was visiting very well kept, but had shocked everyone by randomly opening the drawer of a table. The drawer almost looked like a dustbin, with all and sundry things thrown into it. Everyone in that office starting from the manager got a huge drubbing.

The news of the incident spread in the company like wildfire, and therefore Doshi was extra careful. Dry runs were done for the visit, starting from the main door to all the places that the Director could go to. A minute-by-minute schedule was drawn up and what each person was to do in the complete sequence was clearly laid out and rehearsed. As if it was an army preparing for war, all leaves were cancelled till the visit was over.

With continuous monitoring, Doshi and everyone in the department were ready and fully prepared on that fateful morning. Confidence level was high. The department looked spick and span; everyone was dressed as if participating in a fashion show. All the presentations planned to be given were polished and ready.

The Director was welcomed by Doshi at the entrance of the department as he arrived at the appointed hour. Punctuality was one of his well-known characteristics, a rather uncommon one in India during that time. The Director was six feet tall and had a stern round face with very penetrating eyes. He was impeccably dressed in a light blue suit, which still made him exude the power generally attributed to dark suits. Gold cufflinks were clearly visible on the starched cuffs of his white shirt and he was wearing a matching gold tie pin. His liveried chauffeur walked a few feet behind him carrying his briefcase.

Accompanying Doshi were a couple of his senior officers who shook hands by turns as Doshi called out their names softly, rather mumbled them, and the Director strained hard taking his ears close to Doshi to hear him. He crisply repeated each name that was told to him and looked straight at the person's face, while most of them in turn looked down at his shining black shoes. A bouquet of flowers was given to him by a lady staff member.

He was then taken to the conference room and seated at the head of the U-shaped table. The rest of the team present there stood up as he entered and took their seats again after he sat down. Doshi and the officers occupied predesignated seats on both sides, close to where the Director was sitting. There was a short round of introductions with Doshi calling out the names and designations of the other team members.

The first major item on the agenda was serving tea. Doshi had already collected information on the flavour of tea and the kind of biscuits that the Director liked. Hemant, the office boy, brought the biscuits and kept the plates at preassigned spots on the table. He seemed to be walking slowly with some effort and appeared a bit uncomfortable in shoes that he had been directed to wear that day. Normally he worked barefoot and occasionally wore chappals. His face was pale, and a mild shake could be seen in his hands as he kept the plates of biscuits down on the table.

Then he came back with a tray having four cups of pre-mixed tea, with milk and sugar. He lifted the first cup, his hands trembling by that time, and placed it in front of the Director. The tingling noise between the cup and the saucer, reminding one of an earthquake, was clearly heard in the pin drop silence that prevailed in the room. A good amount of tea fell out of the cup's brim and was in the saucer by the time the tea was placed in front of the Director. Everyone sitting close to him saw it and noticed the frown on his face.

The silence was death-like now, and Doshi had an ashen face. He was sitting closest to the Director. He was looking at the cup intently and seemed to have lost his voice. Hemant did not move from his place, his legs too were shaking by this time. Everyone was expecting a boom and a blast, and not having the courage to look at the Director, had their heads bowed and eyes down. "Sir", a meek voice was suddenly heard, "please see the first example of our overflowing hospitality". Doshi recognised Navalkar's voice. His gaze moved slowly from the saucer filled with tea to the Director's face. He feared the worst now. He would have strangled Navalkar, had he been in grabbing distance.

The Director looked at Navalkar, and a faint smile appeared on his lips. "All right, let's see what you people have done in the last six months", he said. It took a few seconds for everyone to realise that a crisis had been averted. Colour started reappearing on Doshi's face, life was back in Hemant's feet, and he started serving tea to others. Navalkar quickly got up, picked up another cup of tea and replaced the one with the overflowing hospitality in front of the Director. As the visit progressed, people started getting a little relaxed and it ended well.

From that day onwards, Doshi felt indebted to Navalkar for life. Whatever reservations he had about Navalkar's way of spending time in the office and his capabilities was replaced by respect bordering on reverence. Navalkar could carry on his main activity without any hindrance.

So let's come to Navalkar's main activity at the office. He regularly had people coming to meet him, from within the department and rest of the company. All visitors were treated with sweets, as he invariably had a box that someone had given to him. The purpose of these visits was to get his prediction on whether the forthcoming baby in the family will be a boy or a girl.

The expectant mothers or their husbands came to seek Navalkar's expert opinion. After an intent gaze on the person's palm, followed by a minute of deep thought, Navalkar came out with the prediction. Then Navalkar would whisper a word in the ears of the visitor. Privacy on this delicate subject demanded that no one else heard what he said.

Most of the time people came back with a box of sweets to thank him after the baby was born. The exception was when Navalkar had predicted a boy, while the baby born was a girl. The family's hopes had been shattered, as people in India always prefer to have a male offspring. The person would come to Navalkar, sounding unhappy and angry. Navalkar would make him or her sit down and try to understand what the issue was.

"We got a girl, while you had said it will be a boy". At first Navalkar would tell the person about how big a blessing it was to have a girl. "Laksmi (the Hindu goddess of wealth) has come to your home so unexpectedly, be happy about it", he would say. When the person had thawed and was about to leave finally, Navalkar would tell him that he was himself surprised at the prediction having gone wrong. "I have never been wrong on this in my life", he would say with a grim face. "Let me check what I wrote in my diary when you had come to meet me".

He would then carefully take out a diary from his drawer and ask the person the approximate date when they had met on this subject. He would then shuffle through the pages around that date and locate the name of the person. The word written against the person's name would be "Girl".

"So many people come to me", Navalkar would say. "I cannot remember what I have told each one, so I write it down in the diary as soon as the person leaves". The visitor would be shocked, so Navalkar added "You must have consulted someone else also and got mixed up with what he told you and what I had said". The person would look bewildered, but having no way to contest what was written in the diary, would go away muttering that there may have been some confusion. Respect for Navalkar was restored in that person's mind and in the minds of any curious onlookers – there were many.

We were all impressed by the unexplained power of Navalkar in making these predictions correctly. After a couple of years I left the company to join another one. I went to Navalkar and said that as I was going away, I was keen to know the secret of his power of prediction. He agreed to meet me outside the office one evening. He asked me to promise that I will not divulge his secret to anyone in the office. Then over a few drinks he told me that he simply worked on human psychology.

Whenever his prediction was right, there was no issue at all and people just came to thank him and acknowledge his power. When his prediction for a girl was wrong and the baby born was a boy instead, the person was generally too happy to raise any issue and came to him beaming, with a box of sweets. Even in these cases, Navalkar would bring out the diary in case the person insisted that he had been told differently. Invariably the entry in the diary was "Boy".

"I write down the opposite of what I tell the person", Navalkar whispered. He added that I should carefully try to understand the infallibility of this simple scheme later on my own.

He grabbed my hand, kept it on his head, and made me promise again that I will never divulge his secret. I took that pledge and was quite impressed at the simple method that he followed. I kept my promise and till now did not mention his method to anyone. I know that Navalkar retired a few years back and feel that telling his secret will not harm him anymore.

Indians are strong believers in astrologers and palmists

THE CHANGE

Rajeev Lal

The software services industry in India was in its nascent stages in early 1980s. There was still a "Licence Raj", and import of computers required import licences. There were very stringent controls on grant of foreign exchange. The government had just started encouraging the export of software services, and computers could be imported by getting an import licence, which was granted based on commitment to export software in excess of the value imported.

A number of large companies wanted to use powerful computers, but none was available in the market. They were not allowed to import. At the same time, a number of software export companies were looking for a stable revenue support in India that could sustain them while they ventured overseas and grew their business. If they imported computers by getting a licence, they could hire out computer time to users in India within certain limits. This led to a number of arrangements wherein a software exporter signed up with a large Indian user to import a computer that met the latter's needs and software company could get regular revenues by renting it out.

I was working in a large Indian company, a subsidiary of a European global corporation, which was on the lookout for such a solution. We got offers from five to six software export firms, each offering time on a different model of computer. After a detailed commercial and technical evaluation, we shortlisted two. One was an offer for an IBM mainframe, a model that our principals preferred, from a large and financially sound conglomerate. The other was for a new American mini-computer which had suddenly become very popular, from a small company floated by software professionals.

After a series of discussions, we zeroed in on the mini-computer. Their final quote was lower. One morning we called in the young CEO of the proposing company and communicated our decision. He was delighted. My Director was an upright and straightforward person and said to me after the meeting, "now that we have reached a decision, we should inform the other party too about it. You call them up and inform them".

I did so. Within half an hour there was a call back from them saying that they will better the commercial offer of the other party by 5%, whatever it was. I was in a dilemma, more so because the computer that they were offering was clearly the choice of our principals. I went back to the Director. "A verbal commitment is as good as a contract. We have made a commitment – there is no going back on it", he said.

I admired him for his ethical approach, not getting swayed by the prospect of saving some money. In any case both of us were unhappy with the other party for their veiled hints of personal favours in case they were chosen. I called them back and told them that the issue was closed, as we had already made a commitment to the chosen vendor.

Rao, the young CEO of the chosen vendor, started having a series of discussions with us to work out the total plan. He also hired a small office in the city and set up his company's operation. He often took our help and suggestions as he had been working overseas for about seven years and did not have many contacts in the city. He had the idealism of youth, which came out in various discussions.

I had been interfacing with him continuously. The only phone contact we had with him used to be through a phone that he had at home. After he set up the office, he started operating from there. He applied for phones with the government service provider, the only one available at that time, and got sanction for a preferential connection for the business. Almost after three weeks of the sanction, the phone at his office was not installed. I asked him about the delay. He very hesitatingly said, "the lineman who has to install the phone wants some money, and he wants it in advance. I do not mind giving a tip to him after he has done the work to our satisfaction. But I will not agree to his demand for money in advance. It is wrong – and unfair".

I was used to these kind of happenings in every government department and did not even think about it anymore. It was far more convenient to give some bribe and get the work done quicker rather than suffer by being principled. I was tempted to advise Rao to do the same.

But for some reason I held back. If there was someone who wanted to change a bad practice, even in a small way, I did not want to discourage him. Rao spent more money and time meeting the officers in the telephone department but ultimately got his office telephones installed without paying the lineman the money he was asking for in advance. He however, gave a good tip to the lineman after he completed the work. I felt that more persons like him were needed to help change the country.

After our initial deliberations, a configuration for the computer had been agreed upon. The vendor submitted his application for import licence with full detail of the configuration. The import licence applications took about six months to get approved.

About four months after submitting the import

licence application, Rao came to tell us that better technology was available and prices too had fallen in the US due to competition. They could get a computer with higher configuration and storage at the same price. He said that it would mean a delay of about one month as the application had to be amended and approved again. We agreed to his suggestion and communicated it to him through a letter

A week later Rao called from Delhi. He was a bit agitated.

"I do not understand the systems followed in our country. I thought the government will be happy that the country is getting a more powerful computer with the same foreign exchange outflow. It should encourage such changes in import applications. But you know, the concerned clerk is asking for a lac (a hundred thousand) of Rupees to make the change," Rao said, practically in a single breath. He sounded exasperated. The amount was not very high, but the thought of paying a bribe for a genuine transaction was revolting to him.

I understood the reason for his exasperation. A change of mood was needed.

"Rao, can there be a simpler system anywhere in the world? You can pay money and get whatever change you want – whether it is for the better or worse. You are assured of the change. Can there be a simpler system?" I laughed heartily as I said it. Rao understood that there was nothing I could suggest to him. He also laughed.

"Can there be a simpler system anywhere in the world? You can pay money and get whatever change you want – whether it is for the better or worse. You are assured of the change. Can there be a simpler system?" I laughed heartily as I said it.

Rao stuck to his principles. He called me again in the evening. " I am not giving the application for change in configuration. Will you accept the old configuration? " he asked.

This time again I felt that I should support him in his cause. "No issues," I told him." We had anyway agreed to it earlier". Rao did not pay the clerk and came back without submitting the application for change in configuration. In the end the country and all of us lost. That's the way government mostly worked.

Over the years, the software companies set up by young professionals like Rao became the leaders in corporate governance and transparency in India and blazed a new trail. The government in its eagerness to boost the industry made many changes in procedures wherein voluntary disclosures were accepted without inspection and approvals granted automatically. It was one of the reasons for the spectacular growth of the software services industry in India.

"But then there was the Satyam Computers scandal, " you may ask.

There were a few black sheep- they fell off on the way. In case of Satyam Computers, as there would have been a huge impact on the future of the Indian software services industry, government intervened timely in an exceptional manner to protect the interests of customers and employees. A final resolution was done through its sale to another IT services company.

Indian bureaucracy followed a set pattern, it is changing slowly

THE MAN FROM MARS

Rajeev Lal

The farewell lunch for a lady from our department leaving the company had been organised at a nearby restaurant. It was well known for its Mughlai food, but was a multi-cuisine restaurant and with Chinese food also on the menu.

Anant Bhagnani had been in the department for a long time. I always noticed a peculiar smile on the faces of my colleagues whenever his name came up in a discussion – they looked amused. He was at a different location, and I had very little contact with him. He was in the twenty-five member party at the farewell lunch. As always, he was one of the best dressed in the group and greeted everyone with his impeccable manners, more British than Indian.

A medley of Indian dishes were ordered for the group to share, but Anant said he would order for himself. After the steward took the order for the group, he walked over to Anant. People were curious about his exclusive order, wondering why. After a complete scan of the menu, he ordered Egg

Fu Yong. Babu, another old timer, teased him with a smile. "Anant, I thought Egg Fu Yong is like an omelette. Is it normally taken at breakfast?" "No", retorted Anant with a straight no nonsense face, "one can have a Fu Yong with any meal".

We had some beer and cold drinks, and then the food was served. People started eating, and so did Anant. He hailed the waiter after his first bite. "This is not Egg Fu Yong", boomed Anant. All on the table looked towards him. The waiter politely told him that he will take it back and ask the cook to make another one.

We went back to eating our lunch. The waiter came back rather quickly with the changed Egg Fu Yong. This time he kept standing near Anant after serving part of it in his plate, to make sure that he has a satisfied customer. "This too is not Egg Fu Yong", was the mumbling heard by everyone while the bite was still in Anant's mouth. The waiter sought the help of the steward, who also wanted a satisfied customer.

He asked the waiter to call the Chef, who also came quite fast. "Sir, I believe that you did not like our Egg Fu Yong", he said. "The question is not of like or dislike", Anant said sternly, "what you have made is not Egg Fu Yong". "I can make it differently for you, if you tell me how you want it", the chef said.

"I am not here to teach you cooking, you should

know how to make an Egg Fu Yong", responded Anant. " Sir, recipes can vary for place to place; if you tell me what change you want, we will make it again for you".

"I am sorry, I am not here to teach you how to make Fu Yong" Anant repeated, staring at the cook. The old timers in the department had the " here we go again" look by this time. Everyone had stopped eating. Babu intervened to break the stalemate. "Anant, we know now that these people do not know how to make an Egg Fu Yong. Why don't you order something else".

Anant looked around to see if this would make him lose face. He realised that he had brought the party to a standstill. After a pause, he asked for some fried rice instead. The steward, chef and the waiter apologised and withdrew quickly, taking the offending Egg Fu Yong with them. Everyone started eating again, hoping to finish before the fired rice was served.

The group started making movements for a pack-up by the time the fried rice was served. The prospect of having to eat alone forced Anant to eat the dish that was served, this time with a delay which seemed intentional, and we will never know if it was fried rice.

I had some sympathy for Anant as we prepared to leave, and I had some small talk with him about his work etc. I asked him about his family too – wife and children. Suddenly the look on his face was as if I had thrust a knife into him. Babu was in earshot and immediately barged in and changed the subject. After some time we said good bye, conveyed our best wishes again to the lady for whom the farewell had been arranged, and dispersed.

Later in the afternoon I called Babu and asked him about the reason why he had intervened suddenly in my talk with Anant. "Everyone knows that the mention of marriage upsets Anant a lot", he said. Anticipating my follow up question, he continued with the story.

Anant was already in his early thirties a few years back and keen to get married. Normally, a reserved person at office, he suddenly started looking very cheerful. People did not have to wait long to know the reason – he told a few friends on a Friday that he will be getting married over the weekend. The girl was good-looking and very intelligent. Strangely, he did not invite anyone from the office to his marriage and just applied for a week's leave at the end of the day.

He was away for a week and was naturally mobbed when he came to office after a week. The cheer had gone. He had turned more morose than what he had been earlier. There was gossip and guesses around his inability to handle the initial challenges of married life. The anxiety turned to concern when he did not come to the office on

Tuesday. There was no news from him for two days. On Thursday he reappeared, crestfallen and on the verge of a nervous breakdown. He did not speak to anyone.

Post-lunch a couple of his friends decided that they needed to intervene and help. After a lot of pestering, he broke down and narrated what had happened. It seems that within a couple of days of marriage he realised that the lifestyle and habits of his new wife were too extravagant for him to cope with.

On top of it, she began taunting him for his small means and made him feel like a fraudster who had tricked her into marriage with him. Still he tried to take all of it and hope that time would help in getting over the problems, and that she would see reason. He spent the week trying to make her feel at ease and see his point of view. He believed that he was succeeding, but he was in for a shock.

When he reached home on Monday evening, his wife was missing, and the house had been ransacked. All the valuables, expensive electronic items etc. were gone. He spent the next two days trying without success to locate his runaway wife, following all the leads he could get. He was not willing to go to the police, as he felt that nothing would come out of it while he would have further embarrassment. "She even took away the real fancy taps and bathroom fittings that I had", he wailed.

The irony of his grief for the lost plumbing far in excess of the loss of his wife was not lost upon his friends. They controlled their laughter with great difficulty. They consoled him saying that at least the ordeal was short-lived, and he should just forget about the whole thing and move on. It was not easy for Anant, but he did manage to get over it.

The irony of his grief for the lost plumbing far in excess of the loss of his wife was not lost upon his friends.

He was relieved that the episode ended even before he could get his personnel records in the company updated about his marriage.

Over time, he replaced the lost plumbing and the things at home, but vowed never to risk getting married again. Yet, the very mention of his wife or family filled him with grief and anger which he found it impossible to hide or control.

Indians too can be finicky

WHEN IN ROME

Rajeev Lal

When in India, do as the Indians say. Many a time visitors, especially from developed countries, do not follow this. The miseries that befall them are bitter lessons, unforgettable at times.

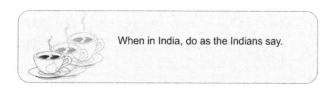

When in India, do as the Indians say.

John was working at Houston in the software lab of a well-known American company. He had never travelled outside the United States. We had a peculiar software bug in the ERP system that we were using, and he was the specialist assigned to solve it. We booked a room for him in a hotel overlooking the Juhu beach in Mumbai. He was different from other Americans we had worked with – extremely formal and soft spoken.

Yet he seemed to have the spirit of adventure. He

enquired whether it was safe for him to stroll on the beach outside his hotel. We advised him not to carry much money, avoid any lonely spot, and ignore anyone trying to help him out of the way. As we had noticed his keenness to try out Indian food, we also told him not to eat anything on the beach which had a string of hawker shops with a variety of eats. We also wanted to send a person to accompany him, but he politely but firmly refused.

When our person went to pick him up next morning to bring him to the office, John did not come down to the hotel reception. He contacted John on phone and John said that he was sick. He refused the offer of our person to visit his room and see if he needed any help. We then spoke to John from the office.

We could gauge from his voice itself that he was very unwell. He had been to the beach previous evening and enjoyed his stroll. On the way back he saw a string of hawker joints and scores of people heartily eating there and enjoying the food. The adventurous spirit overruled the caution that we had given, and John decided to try something new.

He saw a crowded stall with the board saying "Special Pani Puri". Pani-puris are mini-pancakes made of wheat flour that are swelled up into small hollow balls by frying them in oil. At the time of serving, a hole is punched on the top, and then it is filled up with a small quantity of mashed potatoes and cooked chickpeas. It is then filled up with spiced water by dipping it into a large earthenware pot containing the same. The spice content is very high, and chillies are included in the mix. Pani-puri is eaten by putting the filled up ball straight into the mouth in one go. In his enthusiasm to try these, John even ignored that the person was filling the pani-puri using bare hands. It was so spicy that he could not stop after the first one and had eight or ten of them.

Pani-puri can give serious stomach trouble to most Indians, who have much higher immunity to bacteria. An American who had lived in a highly "safe" eating environment can never escape the consequences if he or she tries it on the first day of his visit to India and that too in an open air eating place where hygiene is not a priority at all. We realised the seriousness of the situation and asked the company doctor to go and examine him at the hotel. A colleague from the office also went there to make sure that John received any help required in the situation.

The doctor reported that John had contracted a severe stomach infection and advised him bed rest, prescribing medicines too. He also put him on a very controlled diet. The colleague from our office got the medicines and gave it to John, and called the hotel nutritionist and explained the diet restrictions for John to her. There was no question of John moving out from the hotel for three days, so we worked out a plan for him to work from the hotel to whatever extent possible. Remote working on networks was not in vogue at that time.

John's condition stabilised and improved over the next twenty four hours, and all of us felt relieved. On the fourth day he was able to come to the office. He carried a packed lunch from his hotel. During the remaining four days of his stay in India, we introduced him to Indian food, for which he was very keen, going to known places that used very little spice. It was lucky that he could find a solution to our problem by the end of three days in office. On the last day we took him for some sightseeing at a leisurely pace.

John went back as per his original plan, and all of use heaved a sigh of relief when we came to know that he had bounced back, and the stomach infection he had developed during his stay in India seemed to have been cured by the time he went back home.

John was not the only one who refused to listen to sane advice. Hoshi Yamata worked with the Japanese company whose inverters we had bought (through their agent in India) as a backup power supply for our new computers. He used to look after the installation of high capacity inverters and had travelled often to Singapore, Australia and Hong Kong. He was reasonably good at conversing in English. He had been in touch with us, and we welcomed his plan to come and oversee the installation of the equipment.

Whenever we had a visitor from the United States, Europe or Japan, especially a first-time visitor, we made it a point to have someone from the company receive him or her at the airport and make sure that the person comfortably checked in at the place of stay. We used to arrange for a car for the person for the duration of stay, and the same car, in addition to picking him up from the airport, would take care of all his travel during his stay.

The same was planned for Hoshi, and he was told clearly about it. We asked him for his arrival date, time and flight details. He told us the date, and in spite of repeated reminders, did not send the other details to us, which was quite surprising.

At around 4 p.m. on the date of his expected arrival, I got a call from the reception that a Japanese visitor had come to see me and is on the way to my cabin. A few minutes later, the visitor came in along with an office boy who escorted him, bowed once and slumped in to the visitor chair in front of my table.

His suitcase was deposited in my room by the office boy. Before I could say anything he extended his hand and said "I am Hoshi". He was still slumped in the chair. "We have been desperately trying to get information about your flight", I said "What happened?", I asked with some irritation.

Hoshi took a couple of breaths and started

speaking slowly. He said that he had travelled a lot on work and did not want to trouble us during his visit. He intentionally did not give the details to us and wanted to give us a pleasant surprise by reaching our office on his own.

On arrival he cleared immigration, collected his bags and confidently came out of the airport in Mumbai in a formal suit on a bright and humid afternoon. Services at Indian airports were not as well organised during those days as they are now. He was surrounded by a number of cab drivers offering to take him to his destination and was finally ushered into a yellow and black small Fiat taxi – with no air conditioning.

The driver knew very little English. Hoshi gave him the address of our office written on a piece of paper. He took a person's help to read it to him and then shook his head to confirm that he knew where to go. He drove rashly, weaving through heavy traffic.

Within a few minutes Hoshi was already perspiring and craning his neck to be sure that the cab was not hitting other vehicles or people. The one-hour drive from the airport to our office had him completely shattered.

Reaching our office was no relief; Hoshi could settle the taxi bill only with the help and intervention of some drivers of the cars parked in front – he had no Indian currency. Fortunately he had some US Dollars which the Cab driver agreed to take.

The receptionist later told me that Hoshi entered our office carrying a suitcase, huffing and puffing, and fell completely exhausted on a sofa kept for visitors. He looked dazed, and his shirt was drenched with sweat.

She walked up to Hoshi and offered him a glass of cold water which he gulped. She asked him if he needed any help but he just wanted a few minutes to settle down. After some time Hoshi told her that he had come to see me, and she sent him up with an office boy.

I asked him his first impressions of India and Mumbai. "I have never seen such rash driving", he said. "I was so scared that I kept praying to God all the time to make me reach your office safely".

"Hoshi", I said, "do you know that Indians are some of the most religious people in the world?". "Yes", I've heard so". "Well, now you must have known why", was my retort, "they pray like this at least twice a day." He had a hearty laugh and then we started to discuss the plan for his visit.

Indians are some of the most religious people in the world, for many reasons

THE INDIAN IT PROFESSIONAL

Rajeev Lal

Computer Society of India used to have panel discussions on current topics and issues on Information Technology. In one such meeting in Mumbai that I attended, the chief executive of a manufacturing company expressed his frustration at the churn in his IT team. His last three Heads of IT had served around nine months each. He said that the behaviour of his IT personnel was unprofessional. They would seriously discuss plans and projects and make commitments, and then resign next day for a better salary at some other company or to take up a job overseas.

On top of it, the new manager would completely disagree with the direction taken by his predecessor and would start afresh, leaving the new initiative halfway through and putting the company back to square one. I and others tried to pacify him by saying that in a situation where supply exceeds demand, people are tempted to keep seeking better options. If they get lucrative offers sitting on their table, it is all the more tempting. He was not convinced that such unprofessional behaviour should be considered as normal in the prevailing circumstances.

A similar view was expressed by a CIO in the United States with whom I was exchanging notes on his experience of working with IT professional from various countries. He believed that while Indians are trustworthy and sincere, they are prone to moving to greener pastures at short notice without any consideration to how their exit will affect the project they are working on.

He felt that many of them lacked commitment to the successful completion of their assignments, even though their commitment to completing tasks assigned to them was high. I could only hope that he would have a better experience while working with Indians in future.

While Indians are trustworthy and sincere, they are prone to moving to greener pastures at short notice without any concern of how their exit will affect the project they are working on.

I could never defend the profession passionately, as I too had suffered a lot due to the same reason. Every other month someone in the department would either stop coming to work or would resign with a request to be relieved immediately. He was either travelling abroad, or the next employer was desperate and wanted him to join immediately. What happened to the work that he was handling was no longer of any concern. The irony was that this happened at almost all levels, except the top couple of managers. It was difficult to trust any team member to keep his or her commitment to the project till its completion.

Pramod was a young engineer in a user department where the implementation of a new system was in progress. He was nominated to lead the team from his department. A month after the start of the project, he started coming often to me to seek a position in the IT team. This was a common occurrence.

Salaries in the IT group were higher for the same level of experience than in other departments, people were frequently sent overseas for training and job opportunities in IT outside the company were high. Seeing the clamour, management had agreed that every time there were vacancies at the junior level in the IT department, trainees could be taken from user departments for fifty percent of the positions.

As the prospective candidates had no IT background, a general aptitude test was conducted and the persons securing the highest scores in it were transferred from their departments.

Pramod started attending computer programming classes on his own and offered to work in the evenings and on weekends in the IT department. This was not agreed to, and he was asked to take the next aptitude test. He did so, but was placed at number three in the merit list while there were only two positions available. He was quite depressed. Every evening he would come and stand outside my cabin door and wait till I finished my work, then walk with me to the parking lot, pleading all the way to find some way to get him into the IT department. I suggested to him that having learnt programming, he could even try outside the company or else try to get included for the next aptitude test again. But he kept pestering me. He was so well behaved and soft-spoken that I did not have the heart to brush him off sternly.

Seeing his persistence, I spoke to our Director about making an exception and creating one more position for trainees. To Pramod's good luck, one of the candidates selected from outside did not join. I recommended an exception to fill up the vacancy with an internal trainee, citing that as Pramod had learnt programming on his own, he could start contributing early. This was accepted, and Pramod was very grateful to get an opportunity for transfer to my department.

He was very hard working and outshined the other similar trainees. He went out of the way to seek responsibility, and we were very pleased with him.

Once in a while he would come in the evening like the past to tell me happy he was, how he was contributing with eagerness and thank me again for the opportunity that I had helped him get.

Then suddenly one day he called his supervisor on phone in the evening on a Friday to say that his mother was very sick and he had to go to the village same night. The following Monday he did not come to the office. When his supervisor called his home on Monday evening to check if all is well, his father gave a vague reply saying he does not know how long it will take for Pramod to come back.

Then on Wednesday I gave a ring to his home number. I still believed that Pramod has gone to the village to look after his mother. The conversation went something like this:

"Can I speak to someone in Pramod's family please?"

"Yes, Yes. I am Pramod's father".

"Sir, I am speaking from Pramod's office. How is his mother now?"

"She is fine ... but not well".

"Is she in hospital?"

"Yes, she is in hospital. Pramod has gone to see her in the village".

"Is she serious?"

"Yes, she is very serious".

"Sir, in that case are you are not going there?"

"No, no, she will be all right".

"In that case I assume Pramod will come back to Mumbai soon".

"No. No. It will take a long time".

"How long do you think sir, about a week?"

"No it will take a few weeks".

"Sir, can we speak to Pramod on the phone? Can you please give the number on which we can contact him?"

"No, there is no phone in the village".

"In that case can you please tell me the name of the hospital where she is admitted. We can send someone there and provide any help needed too".

"No. He does not need any help. Thank you".

I could make out that he was not telling the truth. Disgusted, I kept the phone down. Pramod's supervisor, who sat with me as I made the telephone call also understood from the exchange that Pramod had absconded, his mother's illness was a made-up story.

I felt very hurt, as I had expected that the way I had gone really out of the way to help him, he would have not kept me in the dark and behaved the way some others had.

About two months later I got a long letter from Pramod. He had got an offer from a company for immediate placement in the United States. They insisted that he travel in the week that his visa arrived, else the offer would be withdrawn. He apologised for his behaviour and said that he did not want to lose the opportunity for career growth.

I did not reply to his letter. During the next year he telephoned me from the United States but I did not take his calls, saying I was busy. About a year later one day I got a call from the reception that one Mr. Pramod had come to see me, he was an ex-employee. I told the receptionist to convey that I did not wish to meet him.

During my career Pramod was not the only person who had let me down by suddenly leaving the team. I am still in touch with some of those who did it. But I felt so hurt in his case that I never renewed my contact with him, even after his repeated attempts later.

Many young Indian IT professionals are committed only to themselves

STEREOTYPES

Rajeev Lal

I and my family were thrilled to move to the Middle East. The prospect of America-like infrastructure, a choice of the best cars and food and tax-free salary in free foreign exchange allured me to take up an assignment there. The lucrative job offer from a leading business group in Kuwait was the icing on the cake.

This was a few years later to Kuwait's liberation by America-led coalition forces after it had been annexed by Iraq. The scars and wounds of war had practically disappeared, but a lurking fear remained in the country as Saddam Hussein still ruled Iraq.

The unexpected started as soon as I landed in Kuwait. I was travelling alone. I tried to strike a conversation with the person ahead of me in the small queue for immigration who looked to be an Indian. He was very reserved and reticent. He just nodded when I introduced myself and spoke to him in English.

I then tried speaking with him in Hindi, the common language of interaction in India, and he finally responded. "I hail from the state of Uttar Pradesh," he told me. "I have been living in Kuwait for over 20 years."

He was a washerman who used to collect clothes from peoples' homes, wash or iron them as required and deliver them back. He was making good money and used to send some regularly back home to his family. He could not get permissions to get his family to Kuwait; they lived in India and he visited them every year.

"I own a Chevrolet car and use it to collect and deliver clothes," he said with some pride. A car was still a luxury in India. Only people who were well off financially could afford cars.

Earlier, after alighting from the plane I went to a counter to collect my visa. Near the counter I saw a few women from India, most of them wearing saris, gathered in a group at the behest of a person who was putting a number tag on the blouse of each one of them. They had arrived by the same flight.

I later came to know that all of them had travelled on "maid" visas and would go through immigration as a group – handled through the agency that had arranged their employment. I realised that I had travelled with a different mix of passengers on the flight than in my earlier travels

I reached the immigration counter. The immigration officer sitting in the cabin looked gruff and disinterested, except in making sure that my face resembled the photo on the visa and the visa was in order. He stamped my passport and shoved it back to me, along with the visa paper. He waived his hand horizontally indicating that I could proceed.

I had to then pass through Customs. The customs officer was haughty, and signalled with his hands that I should empty the contents of my carryon luggage on the table in front of him. Liquids were still allowed in the hand baggage at that time. He examined each bottle carefully to make sure there was nothing containing alcohol. Then he waived his hand – which meant that I could pack my things back and leave. The absence of any spoken word at immigration or customs was striking.

Krishnan, who worked in the same company that I was joining, and would be my colleague at the office, had come with the office Mandoub (liaison person) to the Airport to receive me. "Welcome to Kuwait , saar," he said and extended his hand for a warm handshake. "My name is Krishnan," He added. I had lived in south India for many years. This is the way "sir" is pronounced often there. He had been given a brief on me and must have seen my photo too as he recognised me easily.

"It is very nice of you Mr. Krishnan to take the trouble to come and receive me," I said as I shook hands. "No trouble saar, it is my pleasure. And you can call me Krish, the way I am known at the office," he replied.

Krish accompanied me to the company guest house where I was to stay till I got my own accommodation. At the guest house I mentioned to him about the fellow travellers while we had a cup of tea. He said that most Asians in the Middle East work as ABCD – Ayah (maid), Butler, Cook, Driver. We then continued to talk about the office, life in Kuwait etc.

Within a fortnight I moved to the apartment that I had rented, close to where Krish was staying. He helped me in locating it and finalizing the lease. I got some minimum furniture and basic kitchen stuff and started staying in the flat. Krish was kind and helpful and invited me for dinner quite often to his home which was at a walking distance.

My wife and son could come to Kuwait after a month and they joined me. I had applied for a local driving licence and was waiting to get one. Hence I did not have a car for myself. For shopping and other work we used to go with Krish in his car. We bought new furniture and appliances including a dishwasher and furnished the flat.

The dishwasher required granular salt to be put into it periodically. We tried at two department stores but could not get it. On the way back from the office one day, Krish suggested that we go to the wholesale market and get a bulk packet that would last a few months.

While the department stores staff spoke English, the local shopkeepers who owned the shops in the wholesale market spoke only in Arabic. We did not understand Arabic except for a couple of words here and there. The Asian staff they hired was mostly from Bangladesh, who understood hardly any English.

We were quite at our wits' end to explain a dishwasher; the closest they could follow was a washing machine. On top of it, salt for use in an appliance was beyond their comprehension. They could only think of soap in the form of a powder. After unsuccessful attempts at three shops to explain what we wanted, the shopkeeper in the fourth one smiled and nodded after we had explained our requirement through gestures. He nodded his head and called his helper, explaining something in Arabic.

The helper quickly went into the warehouse at the back, to an area which we could see from where we were standing. He went up a ladder and came back with a large sack. The only words in English on the sack were "Washing Powder", written in large letters. Both of us burst out laughing, thanked the shopkeeper through gestures and headed for home.

On the way back home Krishnan said, "Our elegant

suits and ties make no difference. The shopkeeper was convinced that we are washermen and wanted to give us the best solution." We laughed all the way back and decided never to try and shop at the wholesale market again.

Next day we narrated our experience in the wholesale market to our colleagues at the office. Most of them were from India. They too had a hearty laugh.

Large number of Asians in the Middle East work as ABCD - Ayah (maid), Butler, Cook, Driver. "Our elegant suits and ties make no difference. The shopkeeper was convinced that we are washermen and wanted to give us the best solution."

Once an Indian, always an Indian

ON-LINE MANAGEMENT – EVENING SHOW

Rajeev Lal

The new customer we acquired in Germany for software services was a very large company. It was a long drawn-out process with a number of meetings over months. At last we were ready to sign an agreement, and a date was fixed one month in advance. It was to take place at the company's headquarters on a Tuesday afternoon followed by a dinner they hosted in the evening. The draft contract was ready for final vetting by the legal and purchase departments of the two companies.

The dinner venue had been decided after the customer Director's secretary enquired about any preference that we had – we conveyed that we were comfortable with any cuisine. An Italian restaurant was chosen, and the venue and the map containing the directions to it were sent immediately, a month in advance of the event. Everything went as per plan, I travelled from India to represent our company, and we signed the agreement.

A couple of managers from the customer side, Karl and Hans, were to visit us the following month to kick off the work. They were coming from Germany via Mumbai and were scheduled to reach Hyderabad at 5 p.m. in the afternoon. We planned to host a welcome dinner at 7 p.m. for them on the evening they arrived. They were open to having an Indian dinner, and we fixed it up at a restaurant close to the hotel where they were to stay.

Their flight from Mumbai was delayed by a couple of hours. They landed at 7 p.m. and were out of the airport by 7:30 p.m. Gopal had gone with a car to pick them up from the airport. The original plan was that he would pick them up from the airport and take them to the hotel. They would have about an hour to check in and change. Gopal would wait at the hotel and then accompany them to the dinner venue in the car. It had rained that afternoon, and there were traffic jams at many places. Due to their flight getting delayed, we concluded that they might not reach the dinner venue before 9 p.m., it may even be a little later. We thought of taking them out for dinner straight from the airport.

"Can we go for dinner directly from here – it's already getting late," Gopal asked soon after he met them when they came out of the Arrivals area. Karl looked at Hans and then replied in the affirmative. The stopover at Mumbai had given them time to rest and change.

They got into the car and left the airport. The first decision we made was to look for an alternative – a good restaurant on the way that they could reach by 8:30 p.m.

That was the trigger for Gopal to begin what seemed to be an unending dialog on phone. He would mention the name of a restaurant, the distance to it from the current location and then the discussion started about the pros and cons of the place. Gopal was loud enough for Karl to listen to all that he said. After what felt like eternity, some decision was made and a relieved Gopal kept his phone down. He gave some quick instructions to the driver and their conversation ended when the driver nodded his head up and down a few times violently.

Gopal was now able to clarify a few things to the guests – why is everyone honking, how come there are buffaloes crossing the road, are four people allowed to sit on a motorbike etc. Gopal was explaining patiently.

The visitors had been listening to the continuous dialog that Gopal had been having and finally Karl asked him about it. Gopal explained that as it would take much longer to reach the originally planned restaurant for dinner, we would be going to another one.

Suddenly they seemed to be stuck – the traffic

was not moving. After five minutes Gopal picked up his phone again and Karl realized that the original discussion had been reignited. New names cropped up and Gopal's face lit up when a decision was reached, rather quickly this time. The ritual with the driver was repeated. He looked stressed initially, but his energetic nods at the end meant that all was well again.

Finally at 8.45 PM they stopped under the glowing neon sign *Cucumber* and Gopal asked them to get down. Hans had been quiet all along. Suddenly he opened up. "This place is different from what was mentioned in our itinerary, " he said. "Such last minute change and confusion in Germany would have surprised annoyed all the participants", Hans said politely. Karl simply nodded. Gopal had a bewildered look on his face.

We had also started from the office for the venue. Every ten minutes we checked our positions. Finally, all of us managed to reach the newly decided restaurant at 8:45 p.m.

After we had settled down, finished the introductions and ordered drinks and food, Karl asked if there was some problem in the evening that led to Gopal being continuously on phone in discussions with us. We told him about the delay that was expected in their reaching the original dinner venue and how we worked all the while to decide and reach an alternate one. We felt elated that we made such vigorous last minute efforts to reduce the delay in starting the dinner. Using our knowledge of the restaurants in the city, we resolved an unexpected problem very quickly and innovatively.

By this time Hans also became curious. He wanted to know how much longer it would have taken them to reach the planned dinner venue compared to the one that we finally chose. "About half an hour", I told them. He looked at Karl and both of them had a big smile on their faces. They found the efforts made by us for the change were disproportionate to the net gain.

We had a nice dinner and then Gopal dropped the guests at the hotel. The traffic had thinned down by that time and they reached there quickly. We went home happy at the achievement of a successful "on-line" change of dinner venue and our high responsiveness to unexpected situations.

Next day in between our meetings I asked Hans if he was upset at the change in dinner plans that we made the previous evening. "Not really", he said. He took out a two-page note that had been circulated by a leading company in the United States advising their employees visiting India on what to expect differently from what they are used to. It was a bulleted list. He pointed to the middle of the first page where the note said "Expect last minute change in dinner venue". "I read this note before I started," he said with a grin.

Out of curiosity, I glanced at the other suggestions. Few that I remember are:

- Eating with hands is common. Wash your hands before and after meals.
- Don't be surprised if a casual acquaintance invites you home.
- Don't feel offended if a lady hesitates in or avoids shaking hands.
- The shake of head may have some meaning. Ask if you do not understand it.
- People in high positions or advanced in age may get offended if addressed by their first name or without a salutation.

Indians believe in high flexibility and accept last minute changes without a frown

HOLIDAYING AT WORK

Bharti Sinha

One of the first things one says goodbye to when one starts a career in the corporate world is holidays. Or rather second. The first is waking up to have breakfast at lunch time and slouching around in crumpled pjs and well-worn to the point of peeping-hole tees.

Such a tragedy!

Finally, when one has a plump enough bank account, there is nowhere one can traipse off to beyond a weekend drive where one competes for parking space, hotel accommodation and jostling at buffet queues, (only to find that what remains is mere dal-roti), and other such jousts with other "holiday-makers", leaving one exhausted and drained and totally unready to go back to work.

Well, the demands of the paapi-pet (or the starving tummy) and the need to earn one's keep, prodded by the innuendo-filled hints from the reluctant-to-support parents, ensures that one is robbed of the opportunity of living life as a proverbial tapeworm. But all is not lost.

If one is blessed with an innate laziness and a crafty mind, and has also managed, through whatever means, to gain a degree professing one is educated, then this is where mother necessity kicks in.

First, one must make a judicious choice, as did I, where travel is part and parcel of one's job description. Opting for Sales, this gave me a much-justified excuse to stay out of office, as well as out of the reach of the bosses, which, believe me, in the days before the cellphone, allowed you the luxury of determining when and for how long you would grace the office with your presence.

Further, you could conveniently schedule meetings allowing you to sneak in those extra winks in the morning or take off for a movie and dinner date in mid-week. With no GPS revealing your actual whereabouts, it was virtually impossible to be caught by falling prey to an accidental or vigilant witness. I know many of my colleagues not only indulged in this freely, but also managed to do business on phone calls even when on tour while lounging in swanky hotel rooms, toting up room service and watching one-day cricket matches. During my career, I have seen many such specimens caught red-handed, booted out and eclipsed into ignominy.

My strategy, however, was not to shirk work.

Rather, I wanted to make a successful career that would allow me to visit places on my bucket list, legitimately and without compromising on work. This friends, is the only way to bring in longevity into your earning capacity.

In the early days, I was a novice having only visited places in the mountains where we trekked and camped in summer or visiting relatives in North India. My very first tour happened on the morning after Operation Bluestar, taking a flight from Delhi to Mumbai at 6:00 a.m., totally oblivious to what had transpired the night before. Being my very first flight as well, I was disturbed by the stringent security check I was subjected to at Delhi airport. Did I look like a potential hijacker, I wondered?

But when I saw all my co-passengers also subjected to the same short-of-strip searches, I realized that I was not special in that regard. Relaxing, I started observing my co-passengers closely so that I could blend into the herd without the shame of having to reveal my lack of experience by asking for directions. I winged it into the aircraft and soon found myself seated in a centre-aisle seat along with three other passengers. Surreptitiously copying others, I could snap the belt shut and ensure I was safely strapped into the seat, when, lo and behold, the penny dropped. The damn belt would not open no matter how much I tugged at it.

Then began what is etched as the most indelible episodes in my memory of the very first work tour.

Panicking but not enough to ask anyone for help, I kept at it, completely missing out on experiencing my first take-off. When the seat belt sign switched off, the stewardess came and offered a sumptuous breakfast. Too petrified, I refused the breakfast, instead still struggling to open the belt and hoping to be spared having my inexperience revealed to all. In fact, a smirking, diamond-dripping, red-lipsticked vision across the aisle was already giving me supercilious glances – to be shamed in front of her, I was sure, would be more mortifying than death itself.

Breakfast cleared, I saw people start making their way to the restroom and the sudden thought struck me like a blow – God, do not make the man seated next to me have a weak bladder. The prayer had not even been completed when in slow motion my neighbour requested me to allow him to exit into the aisle. God, however, was with me that fateful day, for just at the moment my neighbor asked, the red-lipped lady across the aisle used her long-nailed, red-painted fingers to lift the buckle and open her seat belt. A euphoric moment later I could do the same and further declare in a confident manner "of course, by all means" thereby showing off my composure and experience as a seasoned traveller to all beholders.

This experience tantamounted to a good omen for my travelling days. Reaching Mumbai, I went on to take a cab all the way to Nariman Point, seeing many hitherto unseen but familiar sights, made so by all the Bollywood movies, seeing the sea for the first time, the dargah at Worli, Marine Drive and so on.

Suffice it to say, the 5-star hotel I stayed in, the company-paid transportation and meals, and the opportunity to safely explore and experience a new culture and people confirmed to me that this was the life I wanted. Since that day I have never said no to any opportunity to travel for work.

As I increased my frequency as well as places to travel, I learned to make local friends, who brought in an element that can never be experienced through the conjured holiday tours by tour operators. I also discovered that just to travel back to home base on a weekend was expensive for the company and also robbed one of a chance to explore new places. I therefore started using my weekends on tour to both endear myself to the bosses by "saving money" as well as getting that holiday for which I would otherwise have spent a fortune.

The more I travelled, the greedier I was for new places, so I would start by deciding the new destination and then finding prospective clients there. A win-win, wouldn't you say? As I climbed the corporate ladder, this very attitude got my "territory" expanded until "have client, will travel" became my mantra.

This does not mean that travelling for work is without its challenges. Unless one is willing to make significant attitudinal adjustments and stand up to the most stringent scrutiny, this can well rebound on you. One dilemma that always confronted me was presented by the tour policies of our company. We were expected to travel by air, chauffeur-driven cab or AC first class in train.

However, the allowance for food and beverage barely covered the cost of morning tea/coffee and perhaps a dry toast in the super-expensive hotels we stayed in. Again, anyone who visited you from work or the enlarging friends circle would expect to be treated to at least a beverage and sometimes a meal. This meant a deep hole in your pocket. Again, transportation for work was covered, but for personal gallivanting one had to foot the bill.

This continued to mystify me as I always found myself spending money on tour from my own resources. One day, our Head of Accounts decided to educate me, and told me that most people would entertain other colleagues for meals at the hotel or invite a client and present the expenses as legitimate business expenses to the company. This way they could also pocket all the allowances, making some money as well on each tour. I, however, have never been able to rid myself of a black and white perspective in this matter, for, as the elders in my family said, if something legitimately cannot stand up to scrutiny, it is definitely wrong.

However, while my bank balance may not be so fat, all my expenses towards exploring new spots and holidays while touring are definitely a fraction of what I would otherwise have spent. And these also afford the relaxation I would have not been able to get in between the hectic work pressure.

Today, the sight of me travelling for work, armed with a cameras, tripods and walking shoes is familiar to those who know me. And as I notch up the places visited, I am also scouting for new continents, places and adventures.

Who says work-life balance cannot be achieved while toiling hard? Holidaying at work might be a personally expensive tour but is definitely great value for money and a motivator to keep travelling. Of course, provided there is a client who pays to keep you in your employment!

Very few Indians are comfortable with combining work with holidaying

SO FINALLY

This brings us to the end. But no, it should be the beginning. With thousands of companies and millions of people working in them, new humorous stories emerge in India every day. If you look for them, you will find some around you. Would you like others to enjoy these stories too?

Well, then pen them down and publish them. Or share these stories with us. We will include them in the next edition – maybe multiple editions. Your contribution will be duly recognised and acknowledged.

ABOUT THE AUTHORS

Rajeev Lal

Rajeev Lal has written articles and short stories, and occasionally published some of these. At age 73, he has been through the corporate grind for four decades till 2012, as the CEO of a software services company at the end. He lives in India. He worked in Information Services at a number of leading companies. In the last decade of his work, he successfully helped large companies in US and Europe leverage the power of global workforce in Information Services and Product Engineering. He has been a member of a number of professional bodies and held positions of responsibility in them.

Rajeev is a proponent of lifelong learning and is a Director on the Board of the non-profit organization Engineers Without Borders – India.

He is married, with two children and four grandchildren. He has travelled widely. He writes in an easy going style laced with humour, and emotion at times. This is evident in his earlier books "A Star is Born " and "Better Half with Golf". His narratives rely a lot on events and situations that have occurred in his life.

Bharti Sinha

Growing up in the enchanted rolling hills of Sanawar, Bharti Sinha developed a spirit of adventure and a love of nature. In a family of voracious readers, it was inevitable that she acquired an insatiable appetite for reading. This passion drew her to a Masters in English Literature from Delhi University's Lady Shri Ram College where classics were chased down by copious helpings of PG Wodehouse, Peanuts and Gerald Durrell.

When few women opted for roles demanding high commitments towards travel and time, Bharti defied convention. Travelling 20 days a month, she steadily climbed the corporate ladder to top positions of management. With her keen eye for the ridiculous, she observed the spectrum of human nature – a fertile ground for a quick mind and a restless pen.

Eager to push boundaries and explore new avenues, Bharti believes in packing as much living as possible into a day. Hence her diverse activities range from entrepreneurial venture Strategists' World, to advising as a Board member several technology companies, to joining hands with The Sethi Foundation in their transformational Hear A Million program for children.

Living "rent-free" as she puts it, with her mother and three dogs in the suburbs of Delhi, Bharti insists that joy and humour is inherent in the seemingly straightlaced corporate world.

Printed in Great Britain
by Amazon